JOSEPH

FROM PRISON TO PALACE

Gene A. Getz

Regal
Books

A Division of GL Publications
Ventura, CA U.S.A.

Other good reading by Gene A. Getz:
Abraham: Trials and Triumphs
David: God's Man in Faith and Failure
Joshua: Defeat to Victory
Moses: Moments of Glory . . . Feet of Clay
Nehemiah: A Man of Prayer and Persistence

The foreign language publishing of all Regal books is under the direction of GLINT. GLINT provides financial and technical help for the adaptation, translation and publishing of books for millions of people worldwide. For information regarding translation, contact: GLINT, P.O. Box 6688, Ventura, California 93006.

Published by Regal Books
A Division of GL Publications
Ventura, California 93006
Printed in U.S.A.

Library of Congress Cataloging in Publication Data

Getz, Gene A.
    Joseph, from prison to palace.

    1. Joseph (Son of Jacob)   2. Bible. O.T.—Biography.
I. Title.
BS580.J6G47   1983   222'.110924   [B]   82-18571
ISBN 0-8307-0870-7

Contents

WHY THIS STUDY?

Joseph, probably more than any other Old Testament character demonstrates the "mind of Christ." And what is even more startling, his exemplary life-style antedates by hundreds of years the revelation of God's law. He is indeed a model "Christian" in the Old Testament.

Paul wrote to the Roman Christians, urging them to offer themselves to God and not to "conform any longer to the pattern of this world." Rather, he said "be transformed by the *renewing* of your mind" (Rom. 12:2).

Joseph dramatically illustrates this process of renewal. His struggles, heartaches, temptations, decisions and victories speak to every twentieth-century Christian.

RENEWAL—A BIBLICAL PERSPECTIVE

Renewal is the essence of dynamic Christianity and the basis on which Christians, both in a corporate or "body" sense and as individual believers, can determine the will of God. Paul made this clear when he wrote to the Roman Christians—"be transformed by the *renewing of your mind.*" Then he continued "you will be able to test and approve what God's will is" (Rom. 12:2). Here Paul is talking about renewal in a corporate sense. In other words, Paul is asking these Christians as a *body* of believers, to develop the mind of Christ through corporate renewal.

Personal renewal will not happen as God intended it unless it happens in the context of corporate renewal. On the other hand, corporate renewal will not happen as God intended without personal renewal. Both are necessary.

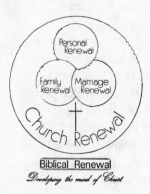

Biblical Renewal
Developing the mind of Christ

The larger circle represents "church renewal." This is the most comprehensive concept in the New Testament. However, every local church is made up of smaller self-contained, but interrelated units. The *family* in Scripture emerges as the "church in miniature." In turn, the family is made up of an even smaller social unit—*marriage*. The third inner circle represents *personal* renewal, which is inseparably linked to all of the other basic units. Marriage is made up of two separate individuals who become one. The family is made up of parents and children who are also to reflect the mind of Christ. And the church is made up of not only individual Christians, but couples and families.

Though all of these social units are interrelated, biblical renewal can begin within any specific social unit. But wherever it begins—in the church, families, marriages or individuals—the process immediately touches all the other social units. And one thing is certain! All that God says is consistent and harmonious. He does not have one set of principles for the church and another set for the family, another for husbands and wives and another for individual Christians. For example, the principles God outlines for local church elders, fathers and husbands regarding their role as leaders are interrelated and consistent. If they are not, we can be sure that we have not interpreted God's plan accurately.

The books listed below are part of the Biblical Renewal Series by Gene Getz designed to provide supportive help in moving toward renewal. They all fit into one of the circles described above and will provoke thought, provide interaction and tangible steps toward growth.

ONE ANOTHER SERIES	PERSONALITY SERIES	THE MEASURE OF SERIES
Building Up One Another	Abraham	Measure of a ...
	David	Church
Encouraging One Another	Joseph	Family
	Joshua	Man
Loving One Another	Moses	Marriage
	Nehemiah	Woman
		Christian–Philippians
		Christian–Titus
		Christian–James 1

Sharpening the Focus of the Church presents an overall perspective for Church Renewal. All of these books are available from your bookstore.

1

Joseph's
Family Background

GENESIS 25; 27-30; 35

- How does family background affect a person's attitude and actions?

- How has your family background affected you?

- Can you think of some people who have had unfortunate family backgrounds but who have not allowed those bad experiences to affect their lives in negative ways?

The main story of Joseph's life actually begins in Genesis chapter 37. He was just "a young man of seventeen." He was out in the field "tending the flocks with his brothers." They were into some kind of mischief and we read that Joseph "brought their father a bad report about them" (Gen. 37:2).

We cannot understand and appreciate the events surrounding this young man's life at this juncture, and later in his life, unless we understand something of his family background. Psychologists tell us that what we are, or were, as teenagers is certainly related to the relationships we've had with our fathers, our mothers, and our brothers and sisters. Even as grown adults, in many respects, we are today what we are because of these relationships. We must certainly expect this to be true of Joseph as well. And it is, but we are also in for some surprises.

JOSEPH'S FATHER
Genesis 25:24-34; 27:1—28:9

In view of this reality, let's begin where chapter 37 begins—with Joseph's father. We read that "Jacob lived in the land where his father had stayed, the land of Canaan" (Gen. 37:1). Joseph's father was Jacob and Jacob's father (Joseph's grandfather) was Isaac. And one step further back brings us to Abraham, Isaac's father (Joseph's great-grandfather). These are very familiar names in the history of the Jewish race. How frequently the Scriptures refer to "the God of *Abraham, Isaac* and *Jacob*."

Esau's Birthright (Gen. 25:24-34)

Jacob and his brother Esau were twins. His name literally means "trickster" or "supplanter," though it is doubtful that his parents gave him the name *Jacob* for this reason. Ironically, as he grew older the meaning of his name became rather descriptive of his behavior.

Though a twin, Jacob was actually the younger brother. Esau then, being the firstborn, was entitled to a double portion of his father's inheritance (Deut. 21:17) and the right to be the legal heir who would carry on the family name. Through a very skillful maneuver, Jacob took advantage of one of Esau's major weaknesses and talked him into signing over his birthright.

Esau had been out in the open field, probably hunting, which was one of his favorite pastimes. When he arrived home he was literally famished. Jacob, no doubt anticipating his arrival and his state of hunger, had already prepared one of Esau's favorite meals. "Quick," Esau gasped, "let me have some of that red stew. I'm famished!" (Gen. 25:30).

Jacob's sneaky plan was unfolding just as he thought it would. He knew his brother's vulnerability when he was hungry. And he knew just how to use that fleshly appetite to cloud his brother's judgments. Consequently, Jacob challenged Esau with something he had probably thought about for a long time. He knew the right moment had arrived. "First," Jacob replied, "sell me your birthright" (Gen. 25:31).

Esau's response was typical of a man who was so engulfed with his immediate desires that he lost perspective. " 'Look, I am about to die,' Esau said. 'What good is the birthright to me?' " (Gen. 25:32).

This response of course was ridiculous. Esau could have tamed his appetite temporarily with some fruit and some vegetables and then gone about preparing his own stew. But not Esau! And Jacob, seeing that his brother was falling headlong into his trap, quickly laid the next card on the table. "Swear to me first"—which Esau did, legally and once for all giving Jacob his birthright (Gen. 25:33).

Esau's Blessing (Gen. 27:1-28:9)

Though we can speculate that Jacob must have pulled a number of additional tricks on his brother during their growing up years, his most daring feat was still ahead. In fact, it was so traumatic for Esau that Jacob had to leave home, fearing that Esau would take his life. And ironically, this final major maneuver against Esau was initiated by the twins' mother, Rebekah. It was no secret that she had favored Jacob all along, whereas Isaac favored Esau (Gen. 25:28).

Their father knew he was getting up in years. His vision

was so far gone he was nearly blind. Fearful that he might die soon, Isaac decided to pronounce his patriarchal blessing on Esau. Consequently, he instructed his eldest son to prepare his favorite meal and afterwards, Isaac promised, he would give him his special blessing.

Overhearing Isaac's conversation with Esau, Rebekah immediately unveiled the most deceptive plan to date—which also gives us insight as to where Jacob learned some of his bad habits. She instructed Jacob to appear before his father dressed like Esau in order to trick him into pronouncing the patriarchal blessing upon Jacob.

It was a dangerous plan. If it failed, Jacob might be *cursed* by his father rather than *blessed*. But the plan did *not* fail. Jacob put on Esau's clothes and even "covered his hands and the smooth part of his neck with . . . goatskins" to appear hairy like his brother Esau (Gen. 27:16). Though he had difficulty faking Esau's voice, Isaac was still deceived and pronounced his blessing on Jacob. The depth and seriousness of this deception are obvious when Jacob had to lie to his father by attributing to God his ability to provide the food so quickly (Gen. 27:20). This aspect of the deception bordered on blasphemy.

When Esau returned from the fields with food, both he and his father Isaac quickly discerned what had happened. But it was too late. The blessing was Jacob's, and Esau, livid with anger, began to plot his brother's death.

Once again Rebekah came to Jacob's side. She conjured up another deceptive plan whereby Jacob could go and live in Haran with her brother Laban. As so often happens, the consequences of one sinful act lead to another. "I'm disgusted with living because of these Hittite women," she said to Isaac. "If Jacob takes a wife from among the women of this land, from Hittite women like these, my life will not be worth living" (Gen. 27:46).

Isaac once again was deceived. Her strategy worked—which is not the first or last time a wife has manipulated her husband with an emotional ploy. He agreed that Jacob should be sent off to Haran to find a wife from "among the daughters of Laban" (Gen. 28:2), not realizing that Rebekah's plan was designed primarily to protect Jacob from Esau.

JOSEPH'S MOTHER
Genesis 29:1–30

When Jacob arrived in the vicinity of Haran, he met some shepherds who were acquainted with his Uncle Laban. They had come to water their own sheep at a large well. While they were conversing, Rachel, a pretty shepherdess—Laban's daughter—appeared on the scene. The shepherds pointed her out to Jacob, and he immediately helped her water her father's sheep and told her that he was a relative of her father. Rachel, excited about her encounter with Jacob, ran home and informed her father. Laban in turn hurried to meet him and invited him into his home.

Laban's Deception (Gen. 29:1–25)

From the moment Jacob laid eyes on Rachel he was impressed. In fact, the Scriptures describe her rather specifically, she "was lovely in form, and beautiful" (Gen. 29:17). Almost instantly Jacob knew he was in love with Rachel. "I'll work for you seven years in return for your younger daughter Rachel," he told Laban (Gen. 29:18). It's amazing how motivating love can be! Jacob had his heart set on Rachel and he was willing to go to any length to have her as his wife.

Laban recognized a good bargain. He consented. And Jacob labored faithfully for seven years. At the end of that period of time, he asked for Rachel's hand in marriage.

Ironically, Jacob was in for the surprise of his life. He was about to experience the results of a deceptive maneuver that would indeed remind him of how his brother Esau must have felt when he was so deceitfully robbed of his birthright and blessing.

It appears that deception runs in the family, for Laban (Rebekah's brother) was about to pull off a scheme that would indeed match his sister's shenanigans. He tricked Jacob. After a great wedding feast, Jacob went to his tent where Rachel supposedly was waiting for him. Unknown to Jacob, the girl in waiting was Leah, Rachel's older sister. Laban had worked out a scheme with her to deceive Jacob. And in the darkness it worked. Jacob was deceived. (I have a feeling he had so much wine at the feast he wouldn't have recognized a total stranger.) When he awakened in the morning, the girl lying beside him was not his beloved Rachel, but Leah.

This turn of events is really quite humorous—but sobering too. Jacob's own deceptive antics were coming home to roost. And this is the way it always is. We cannot use people for our own ends without eventually being used ourselves. Sooner or later we reap what we sow!

Rachel's Price (Gen. 29:25-38)

You can imagine Jacob's surprise—ard response! Now he was livid with anger. The tables were turned. You could probably hear his bellowing voice from one end of town to the other. "What is this you have done to me?" he cried out to Laban. "I served you for Rachel, didn't I? Why have you deceived me?" (Gen. 29:25).

Laban's reply must have incensed Jacob even more. But it also must have brought back some very painful memories regarding his own position in the family as a younger brother, and how he had schemed to gain control of Esau's birthright and blessing. Thus Jacob must have read more into Laban's response than we might think. "It is not our custom here to give the younger daughter in marriage before the older one," Laban replied. "Finish out this daughter's bridal week; then we will give you the younger one also, in return for another seven years of work" (Gen. 29:26,27).

Jacob had no recourse if he wanted Rachel. As with his own brother Esau, what was done was done! And so it happened that Jacob, in a brief period of time, had two wives, not one. This was just the beginning of difficulties in Jacob's family, for the Scriptures are clear that "he loved Rachel more than Leah" (Gen. 29:30). Furthermore, Leah already had three strikes against her the morning after. First, she was not attractive to Jacob. Second, Jacob didn't really love her. Third, she had participated with her father in deceiving Jacob—certainly not a good foundation for building a loving and trustful relationship. Though she may have had little choice in the matter because of her father's ultimatum, Jacob would still transfer his hostility to Leah, even if Laban was the primary culprit. The end result was that there were many years of hurtful dispute and painful jealousy between Leah and Rachel.

JOSEPH'S BROTHERS
Genesis 29:31-30:24; 35:16-20

When Rachel eventually gave birth to Joseph he was the twelfth child in Jacob's family. He had ten older brothers and one sister, named Dinah, and later he had a younger brother named Benjamin. (See figure 1.)

Jacob's Children

by Leah	by Bilhah	by Zilpah	by Leah	by Rachel
1. Reuben	5. Dan	7. Gad	9. Issachar	12. Joseph
2. Simeon	6. Naphtali	8. Asher	10. Zebulun	13. Benjamin
3. Levi			11. Dinah	
4. Judah				

Figure 1

Jacob's Children (Gen. 29:31-30:24)

Following Jacob's marriage to Leah and Rachel, the

Lord favored Leah because Jacob did not love her as he did Rachel. We read that He "opened her womb, but Rachel was barren" (Gen. 29:31). Consequently, in rapid succession Leah gave birth to four sons—*Reuben, Simeon, Levi* and *Judah* (Gen. 29:32-35).

You can imagine Rachel's response and Jacob's disappointment. His greatest frustration was handling Rachel's temper tantrums (Gen. 30:1). On one occasion her intense jealousy caused her to cry out to Jacob, "Give me children, or I'll die!" (Gen. 30:1). Jacob in turn responded with anger and said, "Am I in the place of God, who has kept you from having children?" (Gen. 30:2).

The end result was that Rachel talked Jacob into having children for her by means of her maidservant, Bilhah. This, of course, seems strange and very inappropriate to us, but what Rachel proposed was a very common practice in the pagan culture in which they lived. In fact, certain tablets containing marriage contracts have been discovered by archaeologists which actually specify that a barren wife is *obligated* to provide a substitute woman for her husband so he can have children. This helps explain Abraham's actions when he followed Sarah's suggestion to have a child by means of her servant Hagar.

Understand that these cultural explanations do not condone these men's behavior. We must remember that these Old Testament characters were in the process of moving out of a totally pagan life-style and religious background into a culture that was to be governed by God's laws of ethics and morality. Many years and generations were yet to transpire before God revealed His complete will to the children of Israel at Mount Sinai. And even after He did, some of the most prominent leaders in Israel disobeyed God and suffered the consequences.

Nevertheless, Bilhah bore Jacob and Rachel two children—*Dan* and *Naphtali*. Rachel was elated and her victorious attitude was obvious when Naphtali was born. She stated, no doubt for all to hear, "I have had a great struggle with my sister, and I have won" (Gen. 30:8).

Predictably, Leah was not to be outdone. Seeing "that she had stopped having children, she took her maidservant Zilpah and gave her to Jacob as a wife" (Gen. 30:9). Zilpah in turn bore Jacob, *and Leah*, two more sons—*Gad* and *Asher* (Gen. 30:10-13).

By this time the tension between Leah and Rachel had intensified even more. To make matters worse for Leah, she was excluded from the marital relationship. Not only was Rachel Jacob's favorite, but since Leah seemingly could have no more children, she no longer had access to Jacob. Rachel was in complete control.

But Rachel was in for a big surprise. Her selfish, manipulating behavior was about to backfire. Reuben, Jacob and Leah's firstborn, came home one day from the fields with some mandrakes—small fruit-like apples considered by many in that culture to assist pregnancy. He presented them to his mother, Leah, and when Rachel found out she had the audacity to ask Leah to share them. Leah's response was predictable, "Wasn't it enough that you took away my husband? Will you take my son's mandrakes too?" (Gen. 30:15).

Rachel, desperately wanting the mandrakes for obvious reasons, and knowing Leah was no longer capable of bearing children, consented to let her spend the night with Jacob if she would share the mandrakes. The plan was arranged and can you imagine Rachel's surprise when Leah got pregnant again? In fact, not only did Leah give birth to *Issachar*, but eventually to *Zebulun* and *Dinah*, the only daughter born to Jacob.

Rachel's Death (Gen. 35:16-20)

We can only speculate as to what transpired at this point in Rachel's heart and mind. Some believe that she learned a valuable lesson, and rather than trying to manipulate, control and take matters into her own hands, she turned to God with a broken heart. Whatever happened, God had mercy on Rachel and "opened her womb" (Gen. 30:22). You can imagine her happiness when her son was born. She named him *Joseph*, and her prayer at that moment was for another son, which God eventually gave her, although she died in childbirth (Gen. 35:16-18). The child lived, however, and his name was Benjamin, rounding out Jacob's children to a total of thirteen—twelve sons and one daughter.

The events surrounding Joseph's brothers are about as sordid and shameful as those surrounding his father and mother. Predictably, they were not known as outstanding young men in the Canaanite community. And they were anything but a good example to their younger brother Joseph. This is why we read in our text, that when he was seventeen and "tending the flocks with his brothers,. . . he brought their father a *bad report* about them" (Gen. 37:2).[1] Though Joseph was certainly not above reproach, he was head and shoulders above his brothers in terms of moral and spiritual qualities. In spite of the environment in which he lived and grew up, his life was moving in the right direction. By contrast, he was a different young man and we will see that clearly as the story of his life unfolds before us.

SOME PERSONAL REFLECTIONS

If the Bible were purely a human book, written by purely human authors, it would *not* represent so openly human failures, particularly among the people God chose to represent Him on earth. What we have discovered regarding Joseph's family is, by all standards of righteousness, sordid, shameful, and sad. But it's true!

Why has God been so open regarding the failures of His chosen people? Paul answered that question when he wrote to the Corinthians, reminding them that "God was not pleased with *most*" of the children of Israel and that the judgments that came upon them because of their sin happened to them "as examples and were written down as warnings for us" (1 Cor. 10:5,11). There are valuable lessons in the Old Testament for every twentieth-century Christian. What can we learn from the story of Joseph at this point in our study?

There are two primary points of application that gripped my own heart as I researched and wrote this chapter.

1. I was once again reminded of God's marvelous grace in providing both an earthly and eternal plan for my life. God in His love reached down and chose Abraham, a man who was an idol worshiper, and promised him he would become a channel through whom all peoples of the earth would be blessed. From his loins would come a "great nation" and eventually Jesus Christ, the Saviour of the world (Gen. 12:1-3). Abraham could claim no merit of his own. Neither could Isaac or Jacob—or Joseph. It was by God's pure grace and love that they had any relationship whatsoever with the eternal God.

If God was long-suffering with Jacob and his entire family and eager to forgive their sins and mistakes—and there were many—what about you and me? Each of us stands before God not because of our own works of righteousness but because of this same grace (Eph. 2:8,9). Furthermore, we know so much more about His grace than Jacob and his family could have ever known. We have before us the complete story of His love. We know *why* He did not forsake Jacob's twelve sons. We know that Jesus Christ came into this world and that He died for the sins of all mankind. And we know that through faith in Christ's death and resurrection we can live forever. And we know that some day—perhaps soon—Jesus Christ will come again to take us to live with Him forever. This is why Paul wrote to Titus: "For the grace of God that brings salvation has appeared to all men. It teaches us to say 'No' to ungodliness and worldly passions, and to live self-controlled, upright and godly lives in this present age, while we wait for the blessed hope—the glorious appearing of our great

God and Savior, Jesus Christ, who gave himself for us to redeem us from all wickedness and to purify for himself a people that are his very own, eager to do what is good" (Titus 2:11-14).

2. I was reminded of how easily it is to rationalize present behavior by blaming parental and family influences for present attitudes and actions. This has been one of the great curses of modern psychology. It is true that we tend to be what we are today because of our parental and family relationships. There's a very definite influence, often causing very serious problems in a person's life—even as an adult.

But what about Joseph? He lived in the midst of a family dominated by lying, deceit, immorality and manipulation. If any man had an excuse for turning out bad, Joseph certainly did. He could have easily blamed his dad and his mom and his brothers and even his sister the rest of his life—for repressed anger, lingering bitterness, persistent anxiety, fear of rejection, tendency to be deceitful, manipulative and immoral. After all, he was reared in it for seventeen years!

The facts are he did not. This will become even more clear as we continue a study of his life. Joseph rose above the negative influences in his environment and *chose* to do what was right!

As a pastor and professor I've become quite concerned about Christians who concentrate on their past and blame their family background for their present behavior. Much of this tendency has come from Freudian psychology which still influences most approaches to counseling today. Freud and his disciples often teach us that insight into our past will lead us to change in the present. Unfortunately, they are wrong. In fact, insight into the past—as valuable as it can be—often gives people a reason to continue with immature behavior in the present. The major difference once they gain insight is that they now know *why* they do what they do and they now have a reason to continue.

Don't get me wrong. I believe in psychological insight. It is very helpful to understand *why* we tend to do what we do. And all of us can string out dozens of unfortunate experiences, particularly with our parents. And if we are parents, our children will be able to do the same thing about us because we're not perfect by a long shot.

What I'm saying is that insight per se will not bring change. There are Christians who have been in counseling for months and even years and they still have the same problems and continue to do the same things they did before, only more intelligently.

There is only one basic answer to bringing about change—the *will* to change. Insight helps, but will not automatically bring change. We must determine to do what is right by applying the principles of God's Word. Our goals must be based on God's righteousness. Our source of strength must be the prayers of God's people, the power of God's Spirit, and the encouragement that comes from being with other Christians who live and model Jesus Christ. It is then, and only then, that we will be able to rise above the problems of the past. Joseph demonstrates it can be done!

A PERSONAL CHALLENGE
Are You a Christian?

Have you taken the first step that leads to change—accepting Jesus Christ as your personal Saviour? In Christ we can experience new life by being born again. If you do not know Christ in this way, believe and trust in Him now. The Bible says, "Yet to all who received him, to those who believed in his name, he gave the right to become children of God" (John 1:12).

Are You a Committed Christian?

If you determine by God's grace to become everything God wants you to become, to rise above the problems of the past, you can, by putting on God's armor as outlined in Ephesians 6:10-18. Do not blame others for your problems, your temptations to sin, or for your weaknesses. True, others may be at fault, but putting the blame on others will never bring positive changes in your own life.

Note
1. Hereafter all italicized words in Scripture quotations are added by the author for emphasis.

2

Joseph's
Favored Position

GENESIS 37:1-11

- When was the last time you made a naive judgment? What happened as a result?

- What factors within your environment and within your own personality may be causing you to make inadequate or inappropriate judgments?

- What happens when parents show favoritism toward a younger child in the family? Have you ever experienced this in your own life? If so, what happened in your situation?

We've looked rather broadly at Joseph's family background. Next we want to look at some very specific events in Joseph's life that help us understand some very serious family problems. These events involve his relationship with his father particularly and, subsequently his relationship with his brothers.

JACOB'S FAVORITISM
Genesis 37:3

"[Jacob] loved Joseph more than any of his other sons" (Gen. 37:3). The biblical text is very succinct and direct regarding Joseph's special position in the family. There is no way to misinterpret this statement. Joseph *was* Jacob's favorite son!

Joseph "Had Been Born to Him in His Old Age" (Gen. 37:3)

We also learn why Jacob showed favoritism. He was well along in years when Joseph was born. On the surface this may appear to mean that Jacob related to Joseph more as a grandfather than a father. And this natural tendency was no doubt there. Most parents who have children later in life tend to be more relaxed, easygoing, and to really enjoy the experience more than they did with those that came along in the early years of marriage. One reason for this is that we learn from our previous experiences. Furthermore, we are more adjusted to each other as marital partners and more settled in life. And often we are in a better position economically to give a child more advantages. Under these conditions it is natural to favor a younger child, which can create jealousy on the part of older children who usually have pretty good memories of their own childhood experiences.

Though some of these factors are certainly relevant to Jacob's relationship to Joseph, a more basic interpretation relates to the fact that Joseph was Rachel's firstborn, and Rachel was the woman Jacob really loved. Joseph was the first son born as a result of deep love and affection rather than a mere physical act leading to procreation.

Furthermore, you can imagine the happiness Joseph's birth brought Rachel. For years she tried to have a child.

For years she felt animosity toward Leah because of her sister's fertility. And now, in her old age, God opened her womb. Rachel's happiness and contentment would in itself tend to focus Jacob's favors on Joseph.

Another reason for Jacob's special love for Joseph is that Rachel died about a year before Joseph turned seventeen. Joseph would serve as a constant reminder to Jacob of the woman he felt so close to. It would be a natural tendency to transfer his esteem and love to this young man.

"He Made a Richly Ornamented Robe for Him" (Gen. 37:3)

Not only is the text clear as to *why* "[Jacob] loved Joseph more than any of his other sons" but it is also clear regarding a rather dramatic *way* he demonstrated that favoritism. He gave him a very special gift.

Some translators call this gift "a coat of many colors." However, it was far more than a typical garment with a few added touches of finery. The sleeves reached to the wrists and the main body of the coat to the ankles. And it was beautifully tailored and decorated. It was the kind of coat worn by noblemen and kings' daughters. In fact, we read in another place in Scripture that this kind of garment was worn by royalty (2 Sam. 13:18).

Furthermore, it was *not* the kind of coat worn by a shepherd who needs freedom of movement in both arms and legs. Jacob never intended for this coat to be functional, but representative of Joseph's favored position in the family. It was no doubt symbolic of the fact that Jacob was letting everyone know that he was planning to treat Joseph as his firstborn with all the rights and privileges thereto—namely, that he was entitled to a double portion of the inheritance and he would be the one who would carry on the family name.

How ironical! Years before Jacob had cheated Esau out of his birthright and his own father's special blessing for the elder son. And later he became a victim of similar deception when his uncle Laban tricked him into marrying Leah before he gave him Rachel. Could it be that Jacob was still fighting a battle of guilt and anger because of his own past behavior and experiences—*guilt* because of what he did to Esau, and *anger* because of what Laban did to him? It is possible, for we often allow experiences of this nature to cause us to compensate and rationalize. What more convenient way to appease one's own conscience than to get another person involved in the same kind of behavior—in this instance Jacob's son, Joseph. And furthermore, Jacob's choice seemed so rational and logical, for Joseph *was* the firstborn of the woman he really loved. And what more convenient way to get even with those who caused so much pain than to use one's authority to take away the rights that belong to others?

Even though these speculations may not be accurate in every detail, they are significant and no doubt *generally* accurate. The specific facts are that Jacob "loved Joseph more than any of his other sons" and the primary reason is that Joseph "had been born to him in his old age." And Jacob demonstrated his favoritism toward Joseph in a very obvious way. His actions were by no means unobtrusive!

SIBLING HATRED
Genesis 37:4

The results of Jacob's favoritism towards Joseph is predictable. "When his brothers saw that their father loved him more than any of them, *they hated him and could not speak a kind word to him*" (Gen. 37:4).

Jealousy and hatred are the most withering emotions there are, and they are the most devastating to human relationships. When they penetrate the family they create unhappiness that is unparalleled.

People who hate others find it very difficult to communicate positively to those who are the object of their resentment. And this was exactly what happened in Joseph's family. Considering their own heart attitudes, they certainly were not about to compliment Joseph, nor were they going to wish him God's best.

One-on-one hatred is difficult to deal with. But the problem is compounded and greatly complicated when people are drawn together in "common hatred." They feed on one another's feelings of resentment and collaborate in their actions. They spur one another on. And, as we'll see in a future chapter, this is exactly what happened among Joseph's brothers.

Suffice it to say at this juncture, Joseph knew he was out of harmony with his brothers. They could say nothing good about him nor to him. After all, he had already gotten some of them into trouble with their father by reporting their bad behavior (Gen. 37:2). And now—the royal robe! Joseph was definitely on the outside looking in. The rejection he felt must have been extremely intense, creating severe anxiety and deep feelings of insecurity.

JOSEPH'S NAIVETÉ
Genesis 37:5-11

There is plenty of evidence to demonstrate that this seventeen-year-old young man was very naive. First, he *was* only seventeen. Though a good boy, he lacked experience and wisdom. This should not surprise us.

Second, he was a victim of his father's own naiveté. Anyone with any perspective at all would have counseled Jacob that he was setting Joseph up for some very difficult days ahead. Rather than helping Joseph he was, in the long run, hurting him. On the other hand, let's be realistic! There is no way a teenager is going to turn down a royal robe.

Imagine for a moment that you have a number of children. All of them have given you a rough time except your youngest. He is disciplined, cooperative, sensitive, loving and just an all-around good kid. In the meantime, you've done pretty well in life. You've saved some money. And your youngest son is seventeen, ready to graduate from high school—with highest honors, no less. You're really proud of your son. So you make a decision. On graduation night, when the rest of the family is present for this lovely occasion, you unveil a little surprise for your son. When he walks out of the school gym following graduation exercises, there, sitting in front of the school, is a phenomenon to behold—the dream of every young man. The sign reads: "Congratulations, Son! You deserve it!" The gift? A brand new sports car!

What do you think the older children would be thinking—and feeling—especially since you never gave them anything comparable? In fact, they've sensed all along that you didn't love them as you love your youngest son!

Obviously, in a case like this you would be demonstrating unfair actions towards your older children, no matter what their behavior. Furthermore, you would be doing your youngest a terrible disservice—setting him up for some very unhappy experiences in the future. And there's not one of us who would blame your son for accepting the gift. The problem would focus on you, the father, rather than on your son. And that is exactly the case in the Old Testament story.

But this is a *true* story. Jacob *did* show unusual favoritism towards Joseph. And Joseph, naturally, accepted that favoritism. In fact, like any seventeen-year-old would, he enjoyed it. He also became vulnerable to some very predictable temptations and subsequent reactions.

Joseph's First Dream (Gen. 37:5-9)

Joseph "had a dream." With his brothers he was "binding sheaves of grain out in the field." Suddenly, his "sheaf rose and stood upright." His brothers' sheaves "gathered around" Joseph's and "bowed down to it" (Gen. 37:5-7).

Can you imagine the reaction of the brothers? They saw the implication immediately. There Joseph stood in his royal robe telling them his dream. Their response says it all—"Do you intend to *reign* over us? Will you actually *rule* us?" (v. 8). And the text gives us not only their *verbal* responses, but their *emotional* reactions as well: "And *they hated him all the more* because of his dream and what he had said."

Was Joseph's dream supernatural? Did it come from God? Those are difficult questions to answer categorically. We certainly know from the total story of Joseph's life that this dream *was* prophetic. Many years later, his brothers did bow down to him. But, there are also some very logical explanations for this dream. After all, he did receive a royal robe. Furthermore, he was favored by his father. It would have been very natural for a seventeen-year-old to have visions of grandeur that translated themselves into dreams. And certainly the nature of this dream and the one to follow fits the natural circumstances that were taking place in his own family relationships.

No matter the source of the dream, Joseph was very naive to share his dream with his brothers. Furthermore, anxiety and feelings of rejection tend to do this to all of us, especially if we have been relatively secure and successful as a person. Based upon what was happening in his relationship with his father, Joseph no doubt believed God was going to use him in a special way. It would be natural for him to try to demonstrate to his brothers that what *was* happening was probably what *should* be happening. However, even if it were true, it was lethal—and very naive—for Joseph to share this kind of information with his brothers who were already in bondage to feelings of jealousy and hatred.

Joseph's Second Dream (Gen. 37:9-11)

Joseph's problems intensified when he had a second dream, and again openly shared that dream. The "sun and moon and *eleven* stars" bowed down to Joseph (Gen. 37:9).

If there was any question about the meaning behind the first dream (and there wasn't), there certainly was no speck of doubt regarding the meaning of the second dream. When he mentioned the "eleven stars," the details were *more* than obvious. And his brothers' reactions more than verified that reality.

Joseph also shared this second dream with his father who also got the message very quickly. Jacob "rebuked him," asking him a very pointed question—"Will your mother and I and your brothers actually come and bow down to the ground before you?" (Gen. 37:10).

On the human side of things, we can speculate rather objectively as to what was happening to Joseph. He was already feeling anxious and insecure because of his brothers' hatred and rejection. On the other hand, he was feeling approval and encouragement from his father. He was definitely caught in the middle!

Joseph's first dream seemed to justify his father's favoritism, but sharing that dream with his brothers only led, predictably, to more rejection. He then had a second dream which just happened to include more details. This time there was not just a reference to his brothers collectively, but to his eleven brothers—as well as his father and mother. And the fact that he shared with his father leads to the conclusion he was seeking his father's continual support and approval in the midst of his anxiety. This of course would be a natural thing for Joseph to do in this kind of family predicament.

Think for a moment about your own reactions when you feel insecure, particularly when you feel rejection from people you have been close to. Our tendency is to try to prove "I'm OK."

In many respects, this appears to be Joseph's reaction, and understandably so. Joseph was very naive for several reasons. First, he was young and inexperienced. Second, he *was* a good kid. Third, he *knew* he was a good kid. Fourth, he was favored by his father. And fifth, God *did* have a special plan for his life that would put him in a very prominent position in days to come.

SOME PERSONAL REFLECTIONS

It is sometimes difficult to unravel all the factors involved in a situation like this, particularly when both human and divine factors are involved. But there is enough information in this passage to learn some very specific and valuable lessons. Also, we have the advantage of interpreting these isolated experiences in the light of the total story of Joseph's life, which makes the lessons we can learn even more specific and practical.

1. All of us have factors, both within us and within our environment, that tend to cloud our thinking and blur our judgments. Some of these problems are self-induced. They are purely our fault. On the other hand, some of the factors relate to the mistakes of others. This was certainly true in Jacob's life as well as Joseph's. This is why we must always maintain an attitude of openness and teachability. No one was ever led astray by seeking advice from mature and experienced people.

2. As parents we must be very much on guard against showing favoritism. This is particularly true of children who are born last. In our culture, we usually *do* have more to share with our younger children materially than when we were just starting out. But remember, your older children have good memories. It takes a great deal of wisdom not to, on the one hand, penalize the younger child just because he happens to be the youngest, and at the same time maintain equity with the older children.

Furthermore, we naturally tend to show favoritism to the child or children that are the most cooperative and appreciative. Once again this is a difficult tightrope to walk, since it is not wrong to reward good behavior. But to do so without showing favoritism is a constant challenge!

Remember, too, that your youngest's good behavior may reflect the fact that you've learned more about being a good parent. Older children at times reflect some of our mistakes in their behavior.

3. Teenagers must be on guard against naive responses. First, you are young and lack experience. No matter how much you think you know, there is much that you don't know. This you have to take by faith, but it's true! Lack of wisdom and experience will inevitably lead you to make naive judgments. This is why you need to listen to your parents.

Second, you must guard against being good just to get your way. This is manipulative behavior and often generates favoritism that eventually makes it rough for both you and your parents.

Third, remember that your parents are human. They make mistakes. Don't take advantage of their weaknesses.

4. All of us, no matter what our age, tend to act in naive ways, particularly when we become anxious and insecure. This is particularly true when we sense rejection. We often step up our efforts to prove "I'm OK" and in the process we often experience more rejection. This is particularly true if our behavior is threatening others in the first place.

NOTE: Many people who threaten other people with their personalities, their success patterns, and their capabilities do not understand what is happening. They do not purposely set out to threaten or overshadow others. They do not think of themselves as being more skilled or more capable. This of course is also a naive perspective.

A PERSONAL CHALLENGE

Following are some questions to help you pinpoint areas that need attention.

1. As a Christian, what *factors* in my experience cause me to be naive and to make inadequate judgments?

NOTE: If this question is threatening, it may indicate that you are afraid to ask advice for fear you'll discover you actually need help. Try to deal with this fear by reminding yourself that *everyone* needs help.

2. As a parent, am I showing favoritism? Is this caused by economic factors? Personality differences in the children? Results of my own growth as a parent? Compensation for the mistakes I've made in the past?

3. What can I do to reward good behavior among my children but not show favoritism in the process?

NOTE: Discussing these matters as a father and mother is one way to avoid making decisions that show favoritism. It is also helpful to seek advice from another couple who is working through the same problems as you are. Remember, too, that communication with our children is also a very important factor in avoiding feelings of favoritism.

4. As a teenager, do I seek advice from my parents? Am I critical because I expect too much from them? Am I manipulating them because I know I can gain their special favors by pulling the right strings?

5. As a Christian, am I trying to prove myself by working hard to please others who are rejecting me, perhaps because they are threatened by me in the first place?

A FINAL THOUGHT

If Joseph had been secure and wise he would not have shared his dreams with his brothers. Rather, he would have gone to his father privately, seeking help in understanding his feelings, his motives, and the meaning of his dreams. If he had, both he and his father would have no doubt avoided some serious problems. But even more important, if Jacob had been wise and mature in his relationship with his children, he would not have set Joseph up for what was about to happen.

3
Joseph
Sold into Slavery
GENESIS 37:12-36

- What happens when parents are not in touch with their children's feelings? Has this ever happened to you?

- Why do parents put their children on a performance standard? What often results?

There are two themes that run through Joseph's life story. The first is the most obvious and familiar. *It focuses on Joseph himself.* Even when many of us were small children attending Sunday School, we heard the story of Joseph and how his brothers cruelly stripped him of his richly ornamented robe, mercilessly threw him into a pit, and then without shame and remorse sold him as a slave to a band of merchants who were traveling to Egypt. They then slaughtered a goat, dipped Joseph's coat in the blood and presented it to their father, allowing Jacob to conclude that Joseph had been killed by a wild animal.

These events represent a low point in the behavior of the sons of Jacob. It is one thing to mistreat a non-family member, but quite another to gang up on a younger brother as they did, and then allow their father to suffer incredible mental and emotional anguish as a result of their fabricated story.

The second theme running through this story is more subtle and *focuses, not on Joseph, but on his father Jacob* and why his sons behaved as they did. It is this theme that produces the most valuable lessons for parents. Though Jacob's sons were certainly responsible before God for their sinful behavior, there were some very definite factors that contributed to their actions that relate directly to their father. Though we'll look first at the facts outlined in the passage, we want to concentrate on understanding these facts and how we can become better parents—starting today!

JACOB'S REQUEST AND JOSEPH'S RESPONSE
Genesis 37:12–17

Jacob was a wealthy man. While living in the land of his father-in-law, Laban, he "grew exceedingly prosperous and came to own large flocks, and maidservants and menservants, and camels and donkeys" (Gen. 30:43). After returning to Canaan, Jacob found grazing land for his flocks near Shechem, a city about fifty miles from Hebron where he had settled after Rachel's death (Gen. 35:27). His ten older sons stayed with the flocks.

As time passed, Jacob became concerned. On the surface it would appear he was primarily concerned about his sons' welfare. However, if we look carefully at the text and context of this scriptural record, we find clues that tell us more clearly what was going through Jacob's mind.

The Geographical Location (Gen. 37:12; 33:19; 34:1-31)

The first clue relates to the geographical location.

Jacob's sons "had gone to graze their father's flocks *near Shechem*" (Gen. 37:12).

Several years before, while Jacob was in the process of returning to his father Isaac's home place in Hebron, he had temporarily settled near the city of Shechem. In fact he had purchased a piece of land from the sons of Hamor the Hivite, the ruler of the area (Gen. 33:19). While living in this area, Jacob faced a double tragedy.

First, Shechem, one of Hamor's sons, forced Dinah, Jacob's only daughter, to have sexual relations. However, it was more than a "love 'em and leave 'em" episode. Shechem eventually developed a real love in his heart for Dinah and wanted to marry her. Consequently, he took all the customary steps to try to secure Jacob's permission to take Dinah as his legal wife. In fact, Shechem's father gave Jacob an open invitation to occupy the area. "You can settle among us," he promised. "The land is open to you. Live in it, trade in it, and acquire property in it" (Gen. 34:10). And Shechem himself added, "Let me find favor in your eyes, and I will give you whatever you ask. Make the price for the bride and the gift I am to bring as great as you like, and I'll pay you whatever you ask me. Only give me the girl as my wife" (Gen. 34:11,12).

We can only speculate what Jacob's response *may* have been. But we *know* how his sons responded. They plotted against Shechem and the whole city, telling them they would consent to Dinah's marriage *if* all the men would consent to the rite of circumcision. And while the Shechemites were physically recovering from this experience, Simeon and Levi "took their swords and attacked the unsuspecting city, killing every male" (Gen. 34:25).

Rather than dealing with his sons' murderous actions, Jacob was primarily concerned about his own status and welfare. Speaking specifically to Simeon and Levi, he exclaimed, "You have brought trouble on *me* by making me a stench to the Canaanites and Perizzites, the people living in this land. We are few in number, and if they join forces against me and attack me, I and my household will be destroyed" (Gen. 37:30).

Consequently, Jacob left the area of Shechem, traveled to Bethel and eventually to Hebron. And now, several years later, his sons have returned to graze Jacob's flock in the same vicinity. We can therefore understand why Jacob sent Joseph to check up on his sons and his flocks. Who knows what trouble they may be in?

Joseph's Bad Report (Gen. 37:2,12-17)

There is another clue in the immediate context that helps explain why Jacob asked Joseph to go to Shechem. At the beginning of the chapter we read that Joseph had been "tending the flocks with his brothers" and had "brought their father a *bad report* about them" (Gen. 37:2). We're not told the content of the report, but knowing the history of the sons of Jacob we can speculate it must have been a serious violation of God's standards of righteousness—probably involving some kind of sexual immorality.

Jacob's concern, then, involved more than wanting to know about his sons' health. He had every reason to wonder about their behavior and how this would also affect the welfare of his flocks. Thus he instructed Joseph to "go and see if all is well with your brothers *and with the flocks*" (Gen. 37:14).

Joseph responded immediately to his father's request. However, when he "arrived at Shechem," his brothers had moved to Dothan, a city about fifteen miles farther north. (Gen. 37:14,17).

JACOB'S SONS RETALIATE AND GIVE A FALSE REPORT
Genesis 37:18-33

Neither Jacob nor Joseph anticipated what was about to happen. Jacob's sons were not the least bit impressed with their little brother's appearance. When "they saw him in the

distance" their intense hatred was rekindled and "they plotted to kill him" (Gen. 37:18). And there was no way they
could miss who he was. Joseph was wearing his "richly
ornamented robe." Even at a distance he looked like a
prince, not a fellow shepherd.

Jacob's sons certainly would have remembered Joseph's
"bad report" to their father the last time he was with them.
Furthermore, they remembered his dreams that clearly predicted they would at some point in time "bow down to
him" and honor him as their superior. "Here comes that
dreamer!" they said. Conspiring together, they decided to
"kill him," to dispose of the body by throwing him into one
of the cisterns and then to report to their father that a "ferocious animal" had "devoured him" (Gen. 37:19,20).

Their hearts were truly revealed when they said, "We'll
see what comes of his dreams" (Gen. 37:20). In no way
were they going to acknowledge Joseph as their superior.
And to prove his dreams false, they decided to eliminate the
possibility by destroying Joseph.

Jacob's Ignorance

At this juncture we must make a very important observation. In some respects Jacob knew his sons well. In other
respects he did not know them at all. He understood their
outward behavior, but he knew little of their *inner* feelings.
If he had he would not have set Joseph up for such a bad
experience.

Favoritism, combined with selfish concerns, has a way
of blurring our objectivity—particularly towards our children. This is dramatically illustrated in Jacob's relationship
with his sons. How could he *not* understand what was going
on in their minds and hearts. There are several explanations.

First, Joseph was his favorite son. He was a "good
boy." He was loyal, obedient and trustworthy. Consequently, Jacob put too much responsibility on his shoulders,
not realizing how this would be interpreted by his brothers.

Prejudice, therefore, often causes us to make some very naive judgments.

Second, Jacob was more concerned about his own reputation than his sons' spiritual development. This is evident from the way he handled his sons' behavior when they committed murder in Shechem. Selfish concern also blinds us mentally and emotionally and often causes us to make bad judgments. The fact that Jacob literally sent Joseph into a death trap dramatically illustrates this reality.

Third, Jacob was not in touch with his sons' feelings. True, he was aware of their evil behavior. But, seemingly, he was *not* aware of their inner struggles—their jealousy and their deep hatred for Joseph. If he were, he certainly wouldn't have sent Joseph to Shechem wearing, of all things, his "richly ornamented robe."

Reuben's Disagreement (Gen. 37:21-33)

It is not surprising that Joseph's brothers retaliated. But they were not all in agreement as to what to do. Reuben, the oldest son, disagreed with their plan. " 'Let's not take his life,' he said. 'Don't shed any blood. Throw him into this cistern here in the desert, but don't lay a hand on him.' " (Gen. 37:21,22).

On the surface at least, the other brothers consented to Reuben's plan. When he arrived they tore off Jospeh's richly ornamented robe and "threw him into the cistern" (Gen. 37:24).

You can imagine Joseph's surprise and fear as he walked into this threatening situation. Somehow, he must have thought his brothers would be happy to see him, which points to the depths of his naiveté. Jealous, angry people are never happy to see the one who is causing their negative feelings.

Though the immediate text does not specify Joseph's emotional response, we know from the brothers' later confession in Egypt that he was extremely "distressed." He "pleaded" with them "for his life." However, they showed no mercy and "would not listen" (Gen. 42:21).

In the meantime, the sons of Jacob "sat down to eat their meal," no doubt discussing what to do with Joseph. Reuben—who at this point was absent—had proposed a plan that was only partial. If they were not going to take his life, then what *were* they going to do with Joseph?

Just then they looked up and "saw a caravan of Ishmaelites coming from Gilead" and headed for Egypt to do some trading. Judah, Leah's fourth son, immediately saw a solution to their dilemma. "What will we gain if we kill our brother and cover up his blood? Come," he proposed, "let's sell him to the Ishmaelites and not lay our hands on him; after all, he is our brother, our own flesh and blood" (Gen. 37:25-27).

Judah's conclusion clearly indicates that Reuben's suggestion to preserve Joseph's life was not totally acceptable to the other brothers. The cistern was only a temporary move to pacify Reuben. In his absence they undoubtedly contemplated the matter further. And the caravan of Ishmaelites proved to be a way to get rid of Joseph without actually killing him. At this point they all agreed (Gen. 37:27)—except Reuben, who was not present to voice his disapproval.

Later, Reuben, unaware of what had happened, "returned to the cistern and saw that Joseph was not there" (Gen. 37:29). Terribly disturbed to find Joseph missing, "he tore his clothes." Returning to his brothers with the startling news that Joseph was gone, he cried out, "Where can I turn now?" (Gen. 37:30).

Though the text does not record any dialogue, seemingly it did not take long to convince Reuben to agree with what they wanted to do. They could have their cake and eat it too. Joseph was gone—out of their hair—and they didn't have to kill him. Furthermore, they could explain his absence by following through on their original plan. Consequently, they "slaughtered a goat and dipped the robe in the blood," and then took it back to their father and said shrewdly, "We found this. Examine it to see whether it is your son's robe" (Gen. 37:31,32).

Predictably, Jacob recognized the robe immediately and drew the conclusion they knew he would. "It is my son's robe!" Jacob cried. "Some ferocious animal has devoured him. Joseph has surely been torn to pieces" (Gen. 37:33).

Reuben's Concern

At this juncture we can make some very interesting observations regarding Reuben's attitudes and actions during this whole episode. Why was he so protective of Joseph? On the surface it appears that he had true concern for his younger brother. But if he did, then why did he agree to the plan so quickly to fabricate the story that a wild animal had killed Joseph? Why did he not protest the sale of Joseph? Why did he not go after the Ishmaelite caravan and redeem his brother—no matter what the cost?

The answer seems to be that Reuben's concerns were, first of all, based on his desire to protect himself. After all, he was the eldest, and his father had modeled this selfish trait graphically. Furthermore, he knew he would have to face his father with an explanation for Joseph's absence. And being the oldest, his birthright was at stake.

Second, he was in trouble with his father already. On another occasion, he committed a heinous sin against Jacob. Several years earlier, after Rachel's death, Reuben had committed incest. The scriptural record states it clearly. When Jacob's family was camped in the region of Migdal Eder, "Reuben went in and slept with his father's concubine Bilhah" (Gen. 35:22).

Though it was customary in this culture for a man to bear children by means of a concubine, it was *not* customary nor acceptable for a son to take sexual liberties with the same woman. In doing so, Reuben engaged in sexual intercourse with the mother of his two brothers—Dan and Naphtali.

Jacob's reaction to this event is also enlightening. All we read is that he "heard of it." There's no evidence he did anything about it. However, there *is* evidence that he never forgot it! Consequently, years later when he pronounced his final blessing upon his sons, he stated the following to Reuben: "Reuben, you are my firstborn, my might, the first sign of my strength, excelling in honor, excelling in power. Turbulent as the waters, you will no longer excel, for you went up onto your father's bed, onto my couch and defiled it" (Gen. 49:3,4).

Though Jacob had evidently said very little to Reuben about this matter at the time, the eldest son knew he was already in trouble. And this explains Reuben's fearful statement and question when he found Joseph missing from the cistern—"The boy isn't there! Where can I turn now?"

Inherent in his reactions was the fear that Joseph had escaped. Joseph would naturally return home with the horrible story of what had happened. Since Reuben had proposed the cistern alternative, he no doubt would lead the pack in carrying out the plan. Unknown to Joseph, Reuben had other plans to save Joseph's life. However, we can be assured that no matter what Reuben's involvement, Joseph's report would seriously implicate him in what happened. Consequently, Reuben was scared to death! And this also explains why he also accepted his brothers' solution so quickly. He had no choice—apart from total repentance. Even if he had redeemed Joseph from the Ishmaelites, what had happened would still get back to his father. He would have a tough time explaining his alternate plan—both to Jacob and to Joseph.

JACOB'S DEEP SORROW AND MOURNING
Genesis 37:34-36

Jacob's response is predictable. His deep feelings of

sorrow were accentuated because of his love for his favorite son. He "tore his clothes, put on sackcloth and mourned for his son many days." Furthermore, "he refused to be comforted." We read that all of his children and grandchildren attempted to ease his pain, but his response was pathetic. " 'No,' he said, 'in mourning will I go down to the grave to my son.' " (Gen. 37:34,35).

One wonders how much of Jacob's emotional suffering related to his own mistakes and the guilt he felt regarding his decision to send Joseph to check up on his sons. Reality has a way of jolting us out of our selfish behavior, subjective reactions and naive rationalizations. What a price to pay for irresponsibility! However, the truth remains—we reap what we sow.

But there is another reality. Self-punishment is not the answer! It only makes matters worse. But more about that later.

"Meanwhile," we read, "the Midianites sold Joseph in Egypt to Potiphar, one of Pharaoh's officials, the captain of the guard" (Gen. 37:36). However, that's another action-packed chapter in a very dramatic story. At this point, let's pause to reflect on the lessons that emerge from what we've just studied.

SOME PERSONAL REFLECTIONS

1. It's easy to be out of touch with our children's feelings, even though we think we may understand them. This was certainly true of Jacob. And it can happen to us, particularly in our culture—and especially to fathers. In fact, if it happened to Jacob in a primitive and agrarian culture, how much more it can happen in our twentieth-century culture that promotes the absentee father syndrome. Most fathers in our Western culture are, of necessity, away from their children many hours a week—in some instances all week. And when the father comes home from what is often a very emotionally demanding vocation he is anything but in the mood

to relate to his children—their problems, their needs, their concerns. And if he is not careful, he'll shy away from finding out what their problems really are just to avoid any emotional involvement.

Another reason this happens naturally is that it is much easier to relate to other people's problems than those of your own children. Dealing with these kinds of problems is much more painful when it involves your own flesh and blood.

I really discovered how easy it is to think you know your children, and to discover there is a lot you don't know, when my eldest daughter was in the third grade. She became seriously ill and had to stay out of school for a number of weeks, causing her to get considerably behind in her studies. When she was finally able to return to school I sought permission from her teacher to take her to the public library one afternoon a week to assist her in her studies.

I was amazed at what I discovered about my daughter during those times together—her questions she would never ask in school, her feelings about life, her questions about what she was studying, about Christianity, about her family, and particularly her father. I concluded that in many respects I really didn't begin to know my daughter until that time together. And I'm sure there are still many things I didn't know. But it was a start.

There is no substitute for quality time spent with your children. But it must be time that relates to their own interests and needs—which of course changes as they grow older, and varies with individuals, and certainly varies between the sexes. And we must remember that availability only will not be enough. In other words, it does not work to say—"OK, I'm available! Talk to me!"

Let me give another personal example. My first two children were daughters. When they became junior high age, I discovered there weren't too many things in our culture that junior high girls are really interested in doing with their father. The facts are that a social relationship with their peers is far more important to them emotionally than their social relationship with their father. Those are just the facts.

When they were younger I had taught them to water ski. I decided to use that opportunity to spend time with them during the junior high years particularly. So, during the summer I would often spend a day at the lake driving the boat so they could ski.

However, the secret was that it was *not* "Dad and his girls" spending time together. Rather it was Dad providing an opportunity for his girls and their girl friends to be together. And I spent a lot of time just listening! What a learning experience!

Speaking of listening, I also discovered there are times when a father should sit and listen in other family situations—particularly at the dinner table. There are times he shouldn't even ask any questions, make comments or offer suggestions, unless asked. And even then, he's better off to say very little. It's amazing what you'll learn about your children's inner feelings when they are given uninterrupted time to just talk.

So, what can we learn from Jacob? We may just *think* we know our children, when in reality we know very little about their inner thoughts and feelings. Somehow we must circumvent the demands of our culture and get to know them as they really are.

2. Favoritism often causes us to make naive judgments. Again we see this in Jacob's relationship with his sons. He actually got Joseph into serious trouble by entrusting him with too much responsibility—responsibility that he should have handled himself or at least delegated to a more mature and neutral person.

Today, children often become jealous and angry because parents make naive and unfair judgments, often based on partiality. We must be on guard against this tendency, particularly as our children grow older.

3. Self-protection can cause us to make bad judgments regarding our children—sometimes resulting in our putting them on a performance standard. Jacob demonstrated more concern over his own reputation than he did over the fact that his sons had been involved in sinful and evil practices. When Simeon and Levi committed murder he stated, "You have brought trouble on *me* by making me a stench to . . . the people living in this land" (Gen. 34:30).

How easy it is to fall into this psychological trap! As parents, we can become more concerned about our own image than the real problems facing our children. When we put our children on a performance standard, this creates resentment. Children want to be accepted and loved for *who they are*, not *what they do*.

There is a balance here of course. But if we maintain that balance early in their lives—loving them unconditionally, reassuring them of our love when we have to discipline them—our children will grow up wanting to make us look good rather than bad.

4. Passive fathers create insecure and angry children. Jacob might be classified as the proverbial "passive father." When his sons planned to deceive the Shechemites, he knew nothing about it until it was over. And when it was done, he did little about it except harbor it in his heart and then lower the boom on Reuben just before he died.

This is another trait of passive persons. Rather than dealing with problems immediately, they carry grudges and unexpectedly and much later make the person pay for their crimes. We must certainly avoid this approach with our children. We must be actively involved in their lives *now*! They need correction *now*! And more than anything they need encouragement *now*!

5. We reap what we sow but self-punishment is not the answer to our problems. Jacob refused to be comforted because of what had happened to Joseph. More than we probably know, this refusal was based on the fact that he

knew that he had made some serious mistakes. He was determined to mourn until he died.

All of us parents make mistakes. Some of them—like Jacob's—create problems that are in some respects irreversible. But it does not help to go through life blaming ourselves. Furthermore, it is not God's will that we do so. There is forgiveness in Christ. And if we have sinned against our children we must truly and unconditionally seek their forgiveness. If our motives for confession are to reform them, they'll sense it. However, if our motive in seeking forgiveness is truly godly sorrow they'll sense that too. And then if they don't respond, it is their problem, not ours.

It is improper therefore for parents to go through life punishing themselves, and it is equally wrong for children to go through life blaming their parents for their problems. In fact, no matter what a parent's response, as a child grows up and faces life he must recognize that he is responsible for his own actions.

A PERSONAL RESPONSE

1. To what extent am I aware of my children's true feelings?

SUGGESTION: Look for opportunities to listen carefully to what they're saying, both in their words and actions.

NOTE: Actions may often reveal the opposite of what the child is really feeling.

2. Am I creating jealousy and anger in my children because I'm showing favoritism?

SUGGESTION: Allow your children to voice their feelings without being defensive.

NOTE: What they say may be overstated, but you may have to listen to overstatements to hear what is not an overstatement.

3. Am I putting my children on a performance standard?

SUGGESTION: Never tell your children to avoid embarrassing you, either by direct statement or by implication.

NOTE: Angry children will get angrier when this happens.

4. Am I too passive as a parent?

SUGGESTION: If a father, ask your wife for her opinion. If a mother, ask your husband for his opinion. If you can't agree, ask a friend who will be objective and honest.

NOTE: "Being passive" and "learning to listen" are two different things.

5. Am I punishing myself for mistakes that I've made with my children?

SUGGESTION: Sincerely seek forgiveness for mistakes. Honestly correct what you can, accept what you cannot change, and go on from that point doing the will of God.

NOTE: "If we confess our sins, he is faithful and just and will forgive us our sins and purify us from all unrighteousness" (1 John 1:9).

4

Joseph
Resists Temptation

GENESIS 39:1-20

- When was the last time you were most severely tempted to sin against God?

- What enabled you to withstand that temptation? Or, what caused you to yield?

The focus of this dramatic saga now shifts directly to Joseph. We'll meet his family again, but not until a number of years have come and gone. God's providential spotlight will remain on Joseph for the next major era of his life. Unknown to Joseph, God had a special place for him in the unique and turbulent history of His chosen people. But Joseph could not occupy that place until he was adequately prepared—both spiritually and emotionally. Though the Lord was preparing him all along, in a special sense his intensive education began in Egypt. Joseph had just graduated from his hometown high school and entered the university of Egypt.

JOSEPH'S POSITION IN POTIPHAR'S HOUSE
Genesis 39:1-6

When the Midianite merchants arrived in Egypt, they sold Joseph to Potiphar, a high-ranking Egyptian official. The scriptural record identifies this man as "captain of the guard," but we also know from other sources he was "chief of the executioners." Not only was he the captain of the king's bodyguard, but it was his responsibility to oversee the execution of criminals. He was indeed a prominent man in Egypt.

Joseph's brothers may have forgotten about their brother they had so cruelly sold into slavery. But not Joseph's God! The Lord "was with Joseph and he prospered" (Gen. 39:2). We read "that the Lord gave him success in *everything* he did" (Gen. 39:3).

We're not told what Joseph's first duties were. Naturally he would be assigned the most menial tasks and be under constant supervision and surveillance. But Joseph's character and faithfulness eventually became obvious to Potiphar. What he did, insignificant as it may have been, he did it well. His spirit was cooperative, not rebellious. Though he may have been pampered and even spoiled by his father, he was an intelligent and motivated young man who quickly perceived that he was in a set of circumstances beyond his direct control and he decided to make the best of it. And at some point in time he was assigned to live and serve in Potiphar's home (Gen. 39:2).

What happened is a graphic illustration of what Jesus taught His disciples many years later: a servant who has "been faithful with a few things" will be put "in charge of many things" (Matt. 25:21). This is exactly what happened to this young slave. Joseph used to the full what he had at his disposal and God honored his efforts. Potiphar noticed!

In fact, this Egyptian official recognized that Joseph was no ordinary man. The Scriptures go so far as to say that Potiphar "saw that the *Lord* was with him and that the *Lord* gave him success in everything he did" (Gen. 39:3).

"The Lord Was with Him" (Gen. 39:3)

What this means in every detail we really don't know! However we can speculate on the basis of some well-known facts. Potiphar certainly did not know and believe in the living God who was worshiped by Joseph's great-grandfather Abraham, his grandfather Isaac and Jacob his father. Potiphar was a ruthless, pagan man who worshiped the false gods of Egypt. But in some way he recognized that Joseph's abilities and success were more than natural. They were supernatural!

Perhaps Potiphar saw Joseph kneel and pray to God, just as Daniel did years later when he was in Babylonian captivity. Like Joseph, Daniel was a very successful man in all he did in government circles. One of his secrets was to ask God for help. "Three times a day he got down on his knees and prayed" (Dan 6:10). He did not hide the fact that he worshiped God. In fact, his prayer times were so obvious and successful, other government officials were threatened and jealous, which eventually landed him in a den of lions.

"Let Us Go Up to Bethel, Where I Will Build an Altar to God" (Gen. 35:3)

That Joseph would ask God for help in some *open fashion* is entirely feasible *and* probable. He had a strong commitment to God—as we'll see later in this story—and in more recent years he had often observed his father worship the Lord. Though we've emphasized in previous chapters Jacob's weaknesses, let it be known that he also had great spiritual strengths. This was particularly true in his later years, and especially after he "saw God face to face" on his return trip to Canaan (Gen. 32:22-32). At this point in time the Lord even changed Jacob's name to Israel. This is very significant, for the name *Jacob* meant "trickster," and his new name, *Israel*, meant "to persist with God."

After Jacob's encounter with God, Joseph must have often seen his father offer sacrifices and prayers to God. In fact, when God instructed Jacob to build an altar in Bethel, Jacob obeyed. Not only did he build an altar to God and worship, but he instructed everyone in his household, including his servants and everyone associated with him to "get rid of the foreign gods" they had brought with them on their trip back to Canaan (Gen. 35:1-5).

From this point forward, though not perfect in his judgments and behavior as a father, Jacob was a different man. Even his change of name reflected his new perspective on spiritual values. Naturally, this would impact on young Joseph who was very close to his father.

Potiphar saw those spiritual values reflected in Joseph's attitudes and actions. Thus we read, "The *Lord* was with Joseph and he prospered, and . . . his master saw that the *Lord* was with him and that the *Lord* gave him success in everything he did" (Gen. 39:2,3). It is clear that Potiphar understood that there was a direct cause-effect relationship between Joseph's devotion to God and his successful career as a servant in his household. Consequently, Potiphar looked very favorably on Joseph and promoted him. Though it is difficult to comprehend, this high-ranking official eventually put Joseph "in charge of his household" (Gen. 39:4).

"He Entrusted to His Care Everything He Owned" (Gen. 39:4)

This reflects the ultimate in trust. Joseph's performance and behavior were so outstanding and above reproach that he eventually became Potiphar's executive assistant. This meant supervising all the other servants and employees, handling his public relations, overseeing his finances, administering his agricultural interests and all of his other business activities. In fact, we read that Potiphar "did not concern himself with *anything* except the food he ate" (Gen. 39:6).

Though Joseph's credibility was based on his personal performance, the scriptural record makes it clear that there was another important and deciding factor. Not only did Joseph prosper in all that he did, but "the Lord blessed the household of the Egyptian *because* of Joseph." In fact, "the blessing of the Lord was on *everything* Potiphar had, both in the house and in the field" (Gen. 39:5). Never before had this man ever seen his people as motivated and his crops so productive. It is no wonder Potiphar promoted Joseph to such a high position. He saw he couldn't lose. It really didn't matter to him which "god" was causing all this success as long as it continued. His pagan theological system could certainly absorb Joseph's religious point of view—particularly when it involved material success. Money talks, and Potiphar recognized in Joseph an incredible discovery.

JOSEPH IS PROPOSITIONED BY POTIPHAR'S WIFE
Genesis 39:6-10

When we are the most successful we are often the most vulnerable to temptation. What happened to Joseph vividly illustrates this reality.

Potiphar was not the only one in the household who was taken with Joseph. Eventually Potiphar's wife "took notice" of him as well. However, her motives were quite different from her husband's. Though she may have been jealous of her husband's esteem for Joseph, the Scriptures state clearly that her interests were sexual and she was anything but subtle. Her proposition to Joseph was straightforward and direct. "Come to bed with me!" she said (Gen. 39:7).

Potiphar's wife may have been motivated by a number of factors. Perhaps it *was* jealousy. Or, maybe her husband may have been too busy to meet her emotional and physical needs. In view of the moral value system in the Egyptian culture, Potiphar probably had other women in his life anyway. Perhaps her motives were based on revenge. Furthermore, women in Egypt at this time were more liberated than any other place in the world. The biblical text, however, gives us the most obvious reason. We simply read that "Joseph was well-built and handsome" (Gen. 39:6). He was appealing to her—*and* a real challenge!

Joseph's Remarkable Resistance (Gen. 39:8)

In view of his environment: Joseph's response was remarkable, particularly since he was a young man—and single. Furthermore, she was in many respects his superior, he her servant. Also, Joseph was surrounded by negative examples. Immorality permeated this pagan culture. Sexual behavior in Egypt would make twentieth-century wife-swapping and swinging single life look like a Sunday afternoon picnic. And remember, too, that Joseph's brothers had not been a shining example.

In view of his persistence: Joseph's resistance to temptation is all the more remarkable in view of this woman's persistence. Not only was her invitation direct, but she kept after him "day after day" (Gen. 39:10). And we need not even speculate to conclude that her invitation was more than verbal. She would have used every visual seductive technique she could think of. But "day after day" Joseph "refused to go to bed with her or *even be with her*" (Gen. 39:10).

In view of his limited spiritual background: It is also important to note that this young man's own knowledge of God's laws was limited. This experience antedated by many, many years God's thundering voice from Sinai when He said to the children of Israel, "You shall not commit adultery! You shall not covet your neighbor's wife!" (Exod. 20:14,17). To be specific it would be another 400 years before the Lord led His people out of Egypt back to Canaan.

But in spite of his limited knowledge of God's laws, in spite of the bad examples both in his family and in Egypt, in spite of his own natural desires and tendencies, and—perhaps most significant—in spite of the natural opportunity to cooperate in a relatively safe, secret setting, *Joseph still resisted*!

Joseph's Reasons for Resistance (Gen. 39:8-10)

The Scriptures give two reasons why Joseph continuously resisted. *First, he would not violate Potiphar's trust in him.* "No one is greater in this house than I am," he told her. "My master has withheld nothing from me except you, because you are his wife" (Gen. 39:9). In other words, Joseph knew Potiphar trusted him totally—*even* with his wife. He did not fear leaving Joseph completely in charge, *knowing* he would not take advantage of his wife's sexual overtures—behavior he probably knew very well. Potiphar would have to be totally naive not to know what might happen. This makes the responsibility he gave Joseph and the trust he put in him even more remarkable.

Second, Joseph would not disobey God. Though he *was* limited in his knowledge of God's will, he knew the Lord personally and he believed in his heart that it would be wrong to engage in sexual relations with Potiphar's wife or any other man's wife or with any woman who was not his own wife. He had strong moral convictions and he lived up to the light he had. He would not allow himself to "sin against God" (Gen. 39:9).

But there is one other interrelated factor. An interrelatedness is apparent in the historical record. Potiphar knew about Joseph's faith in God. And he was aware of Joseph's ethical and moral convictions that were based on his relationship with God. For Joseph to violate the Lord's will in this matter would certainly interfere with whatever interest Potiphar had in the one, true God. After all, Potiphar knew beyond a shadow of a doubt that he was blessed because of Joseph's God. For Joseph to violate Potiphar's trust would be to undermine any trust the king was developing in the God who made Joseph trustworthy. Thus Joseph culminated his defense to Potiphar's wife with a very revealing statement *and* question—"My master has withheld nothing from me except you, because you are his wife. How *then* could I do such a wicked thing and sin against God?" (Gen. 39:9).

JOSEPH'S FINAL RESISTANCE AND IMPRISONMENT
Genesis 39:11-20

To resist temptation and be rewarded is one thing. To resist and get into trouble is yet another. From a human perspective, Joseph paid a terrible price for his faithful stand.

On one occasion Joseph entered the house to care for his responsibilities, and once again he encountered Potiphar's wife—*alone*! Not a single servant was in the house, a situation no doubt structured by his master's wife. More aggressive than ever, she tempted him. Grabbing his cloak, she tried to pull him in her direction. Joseph instantly resisted, pulling in the opposite direction. Her grip was firm for he left her standing alone with the cloak in her hand as he literally "*ran* out of the house" (Gen. 39:12).

The results are predictable. Sexual advances combined with overt rejection often generates intense hostility. Knowing Joseph, heretofore he had always resisted graciously, realizing he was her servant. But this time there was no way to resist graciously. Joseph's actions were overt and sudden. And so was her response. Her cries of rage could be heard throughout the house.

But quickly and impulsively she twisted the story— almost as if there had been some twisted motive to begin with. She falsely identified her cause for anger with the opposite of what actually happened. Calling for her servants she accused Joseph of attempted rape. When Potiphar came home she told him the same story, showing him Joseph's cloak to prove her point. The Scriptures state that Potiphar "burned with anger" and he immediately had Joseph imprisoned (Gen. 39:19).

Under ordinary circumstances a man accused of such actions in the Egyptian culture would have been killed. But how much more so when it involved the wife of Potiphar who was "chief of the executioners." A word from Potiphar would have had Joseph's head—immediately!

Why didn't it happen? Why did Potiphar have mercy on Joseph? Certainly God's hand of protection was upon him, for God had a unique plan for his life. But, from a human perspective, Potiphar probably suspected his wife was lying. Perhaps his anger was directed at her as well as Joseph. After all, he would now—to save face—have to take action against the man who had brought him so much success. Considering his own prominent position in Egypt, he felt he had no choice. He *had* to do something. But he *did* choose to allow Joseph to live!

SOME PERSONAL REFLECTIONS

Before looking at some specific ways in which Joseph's experience touches the lives of all of us, it is important to emphasize that temptation affects many areas of our lives. Joseph's temptation was sexual. But it was more. He would naturally fear rejection and loss of position. He *had* to know in his heart that he was in danger of losing everything he had gained. He is a classic example of a person who is "caught between a rock and a hard place." He was "damned if he did and damned if he didn't"! He was in a no-win situation. And some Christians today yield to temptation not because of uncontrollable desire but because they fear being rejected by another person or, in some instances, by their peers.

A single temptation then may have several facets,

touching other areas of our lives as well. But there are also many *kinds* of temptations. One of the most common in our culture—and in every culture since sin entered into the world—is the kind illustrated in Joseph's experience. Sexual desire is normal and often causes people to violate God's will, leading to many heartaches. But temptation also focuses on material things, all legitimate in themselves, but which can become a means of violating the will of God. The apostle John summarized it most clearly when he wrote: "Do not love the world or anything in the world. If anyone loves the world, the love of the Father is not in him. For *everything* in the world—the cravings of sinful man, the lust of his eyes and the boasting of what he has and does—comes not from the Father but from the world. The world and its desires pass away, but the man who does the will of God lives forever" (1 John 2:15-17).

In view of this broader perspective, let's look at some specific lessons we can learn from Joseph's experience and what the Scriptures as a whole teach us about overcoming temptation.

1. When we are the most successful, we are often the most vulnerable to temptation. How true in Joseph's case! And his success was even *caused* by God's blessing, which did not insulate him from Satan.

No matter what our success, we must be on guard in a particular way, for this is often when the enemy of our soul will strike. If he can catch us with our guard down he may at that moment deliver a devastating blow. Before we know what has happened we may find ourselves in a very difficult situation, particularly if we yield in some way.

The apostle Paul stated it very directly to the Corinthians: "So, if you think you are standing firm, be careful that you don't fall!" (1 Cor. 10:12).

2. We will not resist temptation if we do not have firm convictions. Again, Joseph beautifully illustrates this point. He was determined he would not violate the trust placed in

him by Potiphar nor would he "sin against God."

The order here is interesting. It moves from the human to the divine. There are people who trust us not to yield to temptation—our children, our marital partners, our fellow Christians, and last but not least, many of our non-Christian friends and associates. These people trust us. Firm convictions and desires not to violate their trust is a strong source of strength.

The most important motivating source for not yielding to temptation should be our relationship with God. Furthermore, the strongest deterrent ought to focus in His love and grace toward us—not our fear of what He might do or allow to happen to us if we sin. Certainly this should be a factor, but our primary motivation should be that stated by Paul to Titus: "For the grace of God that brings salvation has appeared to all men. It teaches us to say 'No' to ungodliness and worldly passions, and to live self-controlled, upright and godly lives in the present age, while we wait for the blessed hope—the glorious appearing of our great God and Savior, Jesus Christ, who gave himself for us to redeem us from all wickedness and to purify for himself a people that are his very own, eager to do what is good" (Titus 2:11-14).

3. We will not resist temptation if we constantly subject ourselves to verbal and visual stimuli. There is a key phrase in Joseph's story that is easy to miss and yet it is a key to overcoming temptation. Not only did Joseph consistently refuse the invitation from Potiphar's wife, but he eventually refused to "even be with her" (Gen. 39:10).

There are many temptations in our present culture that are generated by verbal and visual stimuli. We can never avoid them all. To do so we would have to leave this world. *But*, we do have certain controls over our environment. For example, what we subject ourselves to, particularly in the world of entertainment, does affect our thoughts, our desires, and our behavior. When what we hear and see on a regular basis promotes values that are out of harmony with

God's will, we are only playing with fire. Eventually we may get painfully burned!

Much of what is happening today is flagrant. We can recognize it and avoid it. But more and more it is becoming subtle. For example, one evening my wife and teenage son were watching a TV movie. It was one of the best I've seen. It was entitled "The Kid from Nowhere" featuring Beau Bridges and Susan St. James and a retarded boy they called Johnnie. Susan played the part of a mother who gave birth to the retarded child and subsequently was deserted by her husband because he couldn't handle the problem. However, she hung in there admirably and became very devoted to the child in spite of the many difficulties she faced.

Beau played the part of a coach in a school for retarded and disabled children. He took a keen interest in Johnnie and wanted to involve him in the sports program. His mother was desperately fearful that her son might get injured.

Eventually, the coach convinced the mother she should allow Johnnie to participate, which helped him greatly and even helped him to win a very coveted award in a special olympic program designed for handicapped children. He showed tremendous compassion for the boy, as only Beau Bridges can exude in movie parts like this one.

But there was more to the story. He fell in love with the boy's mother. Eventually, after a great deal of persistence on his part, they got together for an evening over dinner at her home. After the meal, the coach tucked the boy into bed—a very loving and tender scene—and then proceeded to communicate his love to the boy's mother. She began to respond. Though she did not allow the relationship to culminate that night because of her emotional pain in the past, it was obvious that the value system portrayed was that if their love was real it would, under normal circumstances, culminate in sexual intercourse that very first evening together.

It was *not* a sensuous scene. Rather, it was far more powerful. It was subtle! All along, the coach and the mother had demonstrated spiritual values reflecting compassion and concern for Johnnie and other forgotten children in a way that would put many Christians to shame—including yours truly. And in the midst of that beautiful mood and powerful setting, they presented a scene that communicated that going to bed if you're really in love is what *should* happen. By this time, we, the audience, would be so moved by the overall value system in the film we would have a difficult time accepting the fact that their overall intent was wrong, even *if God* said it was wrong! That *is* subtle—and powerful! And the most subtle part of all was when the coach recognized her resistance and why—and said: "I'm sorry. I've moved too quickly. Can I just stay, lie beside you and just hold you the rest of the night?" In some respects there was more true love in that statement than in any other, but the overall context involved motivations that were a violation of the will of God.

Let us beware! Satan is subtle. I'm not suggesting we should avoid all TV movies. This was a good one—one of the best! But we'd better help our children see through what is happening. If we don't, they—and eventually we—will pay the consequences.

How do we handle temptation? The psalmist stated it clearly:

> Blessed is the man
>   who does not *walk* in the counsel of the wicked
> or *stand* in the way of sinners
>   or *sit* in the seat of mockers.
> But his delight is in the law of the Lord,
>   and on his law he meditates day and night.
> He is like a tree planted by streams of water,
>   which yields its fruit in season
> and whose leaf does not wither.

Whatever he does prospers" (Ps. 1:1-3).

4. When we resist temptation we may pay a price with people, but ultimately never with God. Joseph did pay a price—a painful price. But eventually God honored him for his righteous stand. And God will do the same for us. People may reject us, scoff at us and even tell lies about us, trying to make us look bad. But God will *never* forget!

We must remember also that for Joseph his experience was both a temptation *and* a trial. This is difficult to comprehend, for God does not tempt—Satan does (Jas. 1:13). But God *does* allow trials—often that we might grow spiritually (1 Pet. 1:7), and to prepare us for greater responsibility in His kingdom. And to complicate matters in our own minds, God can actually take evil (which is caused by Satan) and can make it work for good (Rom. 8:28). This Joseph was yet to learn in his future experience.

Just so, God can turn "lemons" into "lemonade" if we'll let Him. All is not lost, even if we stumble and fall. There is forgiveness in Jesus Christ. And we can begin anew. There are things in the past we cannot change, but with His help we can make significant changes in the future—and be at peace within ourselves.

And remember! Paul wrote: "No temptation has seized you except what is common to man. And God is faithful; he will not let you be tempted beyond what you can bear. But when you are tempted, he will also provide a way out so that you can stand up under it" (1 Cor. 10:13).

A PERSONAL CHALLENGE
Following are some questions to help you apply the lessons we've learned from Joseph in your own life—beginning today!

1. Am I aware that Satan often strikes when we are the most successful—spiritually, domestically, vocationally and socially?

2. Do I have firm convictions that are based squarely on God's Word which will enable me to withstand temptations? How committed am I to those convictions?

3. Do I avoid verbal and visual stimuli that weaken my resistance to temptation?

4. Do I truly believe that God will honor my refusal to become involved in sinful attitudes and actions?

5
Joseph's
Prison Experience

GENESIS 39:20-23; 40:1-23

- From your own personal experiences what do you think are the most basic causes of bitterness towards others?

- Have you ever felt bitter towards God because of bitterness towards others?

- In what subtle ways do we attempt to vindicate ourselves when we have been mistreated?

All of us have felt the emotional sting that accompanies unjust treatment. In some instances, the pain has also been physical, but even then, what we remember most are the feelings those experiences generated. Someone at some point in our lives has been unfair. *we have been hurt.*

Joseph stands out in the Old Testament as a classic example of one who was repeatedly mistreated. He probably experienced more injustice than any other biblical char-

acter outside of Jesus Christ. He was scorned and rejected
by his brothers when he was sincerely seeking to find out
how they were doing. Because of their jealousy and hatred
he was physically abused and sold as a slave into Egypt.
When he refused to yield to temptation he was falsely
accused by Potiphar's wife, and then unjustly removed from
his high-ranking position in Potiphar's house and put in
prison. And in this lesson we'll see that while imprisoned,
he was forgotten by a man he helped and encouraged the
most.

Joseph knew experientially what mistreatment really
was. Though difficult to understand, he did not allow bitterness or self-pity to wither his soul. Joseph is a marvelous
example of Christlike behavior in the Old Testament.

JOSEPH'S SUCCESS AND PROMOTION
Genesis 39:20-23

In some respects the next installment in Joseph's life
story sounds repetitious. And it is—by divine design!
Notice the following similarities:

Joseph in Potiphar's House	Joseph in Prison
1. *"The Lord was with Joseph"* (Gen. 39:2).	1. "But while Joseph was there in the prison, *the Lord was with him*" (Gen. 39:20,21).
2. "Joseph found *favor* in his eyes and became his attendant" (Gen. 39:4).	2. "The Lord . . . granted him *favor* in the eyes of the prison warden" (Gen. 39:21).
3. "Potiphar put him *in charge* of his household, and he entrusted to his care *everything* he owned" (Gen. 39:4).	3. "The warden put Joseph *in charge* of all those held in prison, and he was made responsible *for all* that was done there" (Gen. 39:22).
4. "With Joseph in	4. *"The warden paid no*

charge, he *did not concern himself* with anything except the food he ate" (Gen. 39:6).

5. Potiphar trusted Joseph because "he saw that . . . *the Lord gave him success* in everything he did" (Gen. 39:3).

attention to anything under Joseph's care" (Gen. 39:23).

5. The prison warden trusted Joseph because he too saw that *"the Lord* . . . gave *him success* in whatever he did" (Gen. 39:23).

The parallels in these two experiences are very clear. *First*, when Joseph was debased by his brothers and sold into Egyptian slavery, *God did not forsake him*. And when he was demoted by Potiphar, again the Lord stayed by his side. God never forgot Joseph nor did He leave him. He "was with Joseph."

Second, when Joseph began his duties as Potiphar's slave, *he demonstrated positive attitudes and "found favor in his eyes."* Just so, God also granted Joseph "favor in the eyes of the prison warden." He was noticed by both men. He was a model slave *and* a model prisoner.

Third, Joseph was promoted and given a high-level supervisory task in Potiphar's household *and* in prison. In both situations he was given overall and complete responsibility, and was put in charge of *everything* Potiphar owned, and in prison he was responsible for *whatever* needed to be done.

The fourth similarity involves the trust factor. Both Potiphar and the warden turned everything over to Joseph and did not *worry* about a thing. Seemingly, they came to the place where they did not even check up on him. He was totally in charge and responsible. They knew he would not let them down.

The *fifth* parallel is the most important. *Both men saw a very definite correlation between the God Joseph worshiped and the success he enjoyed.* This became a significant factor in forming a basis for their trust. Whatever means Joseph used to demonstrate the relationship between his success and his faith in God, it was highly visible. Neither Potiphar nor the prison warden missed seeing the correlation. Both were impressed, not necessarily because of Joseph's faith, prayers and other religious exercises, but because of the *results* of his relationship with God. This is indeed what impresses the non-Christian who knows nothing of what it really means to live for God and to trust Him in difficult circumstances.

You are an open Bible. Your life is the only testimony of Jesus Christ and what Christ is to an unsaved friend or loved one.

JOSEPH'S OPPORTUNITY TO INTERPRET TWO DREAMS
Genesis 40:1-19

At this point in Joseph's life, approximately eleven years have passed since he was sold into Egypt.[1] Most of this time was probably spent in prison following his painful experience in Potiphar's house.

Though Joseph was eventually given a great deal of freedom along with responsibility to manage the prison, his initial time was very difficult. The psalmist tells us that "they bruised his feet with shackles" and "his neck was put in irons" (Ps. 105:18). How long he was in this kind of bondage we do not know. But we *do* know that it was long enough for the shackles to cause serious bruises and wounds. And we also know that Joseph's attitudes and actions throughout the whole ordeal were incredibly exemplary for one who had been so mistreated by his own family and was now innocently incarcerated by the man whose trust he refused to violate.

The King's Cupbearer (Gen. 40:1-4)

Eventually Joseph was rewarded with a degree of freedom and unusual responsibility within the prison itself. And one day he was assigned two men who were not the average, run-of-the-mill prisoners. They were the "*cupbearer* and the *baker* of the king of Egypt"—representing two very responsible positions. The cupbearer was the man who was so highly trusted by the king that he tasted the king's food and drink to make sure no one would attempt to assassinate him through poisoning. Furthermore, the king usually took his cupbearer into his confidence, seeking his advice on very important matters. Many years later, Nehemiah fulfilled this responsibility for King Artaxerxes (Neh. 1:11; 2:1).

The baker likewise was a very trusted man. He had the oversight of all food preparation. If anyone was going to try to poison the king, it would probably begin in the king's kitchen. Thus no doubt the cupbearer and the baker were close friends and associates. If someone *did* slip poison into the king's food and drink, the cupbearer unfortunately would be the first to discover it. He would be very dependent, then, on the baker to keep it from happening in the first place.

We are not told why the men were in prison, except that they "offended their master, the king of Egypt" (Gen. 40:1). However, from the overall story we can conjecture that the baker was probably more guilty than the cupbearer. In fact, it may be that, since these men worked so closely together, the cupbearer was guilty only by association. But whatever the crime, it was no doubt very serious. They were not just dismissed! They were put in prison!

There is another interesting sidelight in the historical record. Not only were the cupbearer and the baker confined to the same prison as Joseph, but they were assigned *to Joseph* by "*the captain of the guard*" (Gen. 40:4)—who was none other than Potiphar, the man responsible for Joseph's own incarceration. This observation adds credence to the hypothesis that Potiphar knew in his heart that Joseph had never been guilty of trying to rape his wife. In fact, he may have had an important part in building a bridge between Joseph and the prison warden, who later trusted

Joseph in so many similar ways as Potiphar had done.

Note also that Joseph "attended" these men. This indicates they were not ordinary prisoners. Because of their high-level positions in the king's court, they were given special privileges and treatment. And, as will be seen, the fact that the captain of the guard assigned Joseph to look after these men is very significant in God's providential plans for this young man.

The Two Dreams and Joseph's Interpretation (Gen. 40:4-19)

After the cupbearer and the baker "had been in custody for some time," both men had dreams—and on the very same night (Gen. 40:4,5). Furthermore, the content of each dream was so related to each man's vocation and so similar in certain respects that they knew what had happened was not just a bizarre manifestation of their subconscious anxiety and fear. However, they *were* fearful and anxious, more so after the dreams than before. In fact, when "Joseph came to them the next morning" he couldn't help but notice their dejection (Gen. 40:6). "Why are your faces so sad today?" he asked (Gen. 40:7).

The men related to Joseph what had happened, but indicated their need for an interpretation. Joseph's response reflects his own *growing relationship with God* in the midst of difficulties as well as his *boldness* in letting others know what he believed. "Do not interpretations belong to God?" he asked. "Tell me your dreams" (Gen. 40:8). And of course, this final statement also let them know—and anyone else who might be listening—that he believed that with God's assistance he *could* help them understand their dreams.

The cupbearer went first. In his dream he saw a vine with three branches. Very quickly the vine produced grapes, and the cupbearer saw himself squeezing the juice into Pharaoh's cup and serving him (Gen. 40:9-11).

Joseph immediately interpreted the dream; in three days the cupbearer would be restored to his position in Pharaoh's court. But just as quickly Joseph added a personal request. "But when all goes well with you, remember me and show me kindness" he said. "Mention me to Pharaoh and get me out of this prison" (Gen. 40:14).

Joseph went on to relate *why* he was in prison. "I was forcibly carried off from the land of the Hebrews," he explained, "and even here I have done nothing to deserve being put in a dungeon" (Gen. 40:15).

Joseph knew he was innocent and he also knew that this was the time to express it. And I'm glad he did, for it tells us there's a time to defend oneself against false accusations—even though God is the ultimate vindicator. There's also a time to ask someone to put in a good word for us even though we are trusting God with all our hearts to help us and to defend us. But it must be emphasized that timing is very important. Had Joseph attempted to vindicate himself in his own efforts rather than waiting for God's moment in his life, he may never have gotten the unique opportunity that came his way that day. Wrong timing often causes legitimate self-defense to appear defensive.

The chief baker was watching and listening intently. Seemingly, he had been hesitant to share his dream for fear the interpretation may not be favorable to his future welfare. And understandably so! Though certain elements in the two dreams were similar, some were very dissimilar. And the chief baker was smart enough to know that his dream might be communicating some bad omens.

Nevertheless, he drew courage from Joseph's positive response to the cupbearer's dream. Consequently he related his own. In his dream he was carrying three baskets of food containing "all kinds of baked goods for Pharaoh." However, as he walked along, carrying the baskets on his head, the birds swooped down and ate out of the baskets (Gen. 40:16,17).

Joseph's response was just as quick as before and just as succinct. However, what he said was *not* favorable—just as the baker had feared. "The three baskets are three days," Joseph said—which was the similarity with the cupbearer's dream. However, and unfortunately for the baker, there was a dissimilarity. "Within three days," Joseph stated, "Pharaoh will lift off your head and hang you on a tree. And the birds will eat away your flesh" (Gen. 40:18,19).

JOSEPH'S PROPHESIES FULFILLED
Genesis 40:20-23

In three days, everything happened just as Joseph said it would. Pharaoh restored his cupbearer to his previous position but he had the chief baker executed. And, if justice was truly done, this may indicate that it was indeed the chief baker who was guilty of instigating what had happened to get them imprisoned in the first place. Furthermore, the fact that Pharaoh restored the cupbearer to such a prominent position demanding such total trust also points to his innocence. If he had been guilty of any serious wrong behavior, it doesn't seem feasible that the king would have given his cupbearer another opportunity to protect him from assassination.

But the ironical part of the story is that once restored because of his *innocence*, the cupbearer did not remember Joseph who was also in prison in spite of his own *innocence*. Even though Joseph had taken personal interest in him when he was dejected and sad, the cupbearer did nothing about Joseph's personal request.

We're not told *why* he forgot. Was it just a bad memory? Probably not. He may have been afraid to speak to Pharaoh about it for fear he would open some old wounds he'd rather not get involved in. Consequently, he may have just decided to forget. Or perhaps he was so enamored with his own restoration that he couldn't think about helping anybody else. Whatever the reason, we simply read that he "did not remember Joseph; he forgot him" (Gen. 40;23). And once again, after patiently waiting for a number of years for this kind of opportunity, Joseph was unjustly treated. But unknown to him, another opportunity was coming—an opportunity that was far greater than the one that passed him by. It would be another two years—but it was coming, and when it did it would be worth waiting for.

SOME PERSONAL REFLECTIONS

As stated at the beginning of this chapter, someone at some point in our lives has done something to us that we feel has been unfair. It may have been a family member, a teacher, a friend, or an employer. It may have happened at home, at church, in school, or on the job. It may have taken place many years ago when we were children or it may have been just yesterday. It may have happened once or many times. It may have involved harsh words, rejection, a rumor, physical abuse, false accusations, or unjust criticism. Or it may have been as simple as being taken for granted or being used for selfish purposes. And it may have been malicious or inadvertent. In some instances it may have been our own perception of the situation, but whatever the experience it was painful.

The important question is, What can we learn from Joseph's example and how he faced injustice? For most of us, of course, his mistreatment makes anything we have experienced seem insignificant. On the other hand, any kind of injustice is emotionally painful and affects our behavior—both in the midst of the difficulties as well as when it is over. Joseph is a powerful example in both situations.

1. Joseph did not allow bitterness to capture his soul. Neither should we! Humanly speaking, Joseph had every reason to develop a bitter spirit. And there had to be moments in his life when he *was* angry. After all he was human. But there's a difference between getting angry and letting "the sun go down while you are still angry." As Paul

stated further in his letter to the Ephesians, this is what
gives "the devil a foothold" in our lives (Eph. 4:26,27).
Anger that is not dealt with will lead to lingering bitterness
and all the other kinds of sinful behavior that result. And in
the end, we not only hurt others but we also hurt ourselves.
Bitterness is intensely self-destructive—emotionally, physically and spiritually.

Don't misunderstand! This does not mean we cannot
speak out against injustice—even when that injustice is
directed towards ourselves. Joseph did. He very clearly
explained to the cupbearer that he had been mistreated and
didn't belong in Egypt, let alone in an Egyptian prison. But
he waited for God's timing which is always a unique opportunity to defend oneself without being or appearing defensive.

Why was Joseph able to handle this incredible and persistent mistreatment so well? This leads us to our next lesson from his life.

2. Joseph did not turn against God; rather he turned *to*
God even more. And so should we! Many people who are
mistreated allow their bitterness toward those who caused it
to also be directed towards God. They blame God for allowing it to happen.

Think about Joseph for a moment! Though he was not
perfect and certainly was naive in his relationship with his
brothers, in his heart he was reaching out to help them. Furthermore, he was only doing what his father had asked.
And in Egypt, he resisted temptation so as not to violate
God's will or Potiphar's trust in him. And yet, he was mistreated for doing what was right. Do you think he was ever
tempted to blame God? I'm confident he was. But he did
not allow *that* temptation to result in sinful attitudes and
actions. The facts are, he grew in his relationship with God.
He only trusted Him more to be with him and to help him
endure the crises.

In this sense, Joseph was projecting ahead many years

in his difficult experience, and fleshing out the powerful truth stated by the apostle Peter, who writing to Christian slaves in the first-century church, exhorted: "Submit yourselves to your masters with all respect, not only to those who are good and considerate, but also to those who are harsh. For it is commendable if a man bears up under the pain of unjust suffering because he is conscious of God. But how is it to your credit if you receive a beating for doing wrong and endure it? But if you suffer for doing good and you endure it, this is commendable before God. To this you were called, because Christ suffered for you, leaving you an example, that you should follow in his steps" (1 Peter 2:18-21).

Fortunately most of us have not had to face this kind of mistreatment. But how do we respond to the mistreatment we do face? No matter what the emotional or physical pain, we must not allow ourselves to become bitter towards God, for if we do we will only compound our problem. Not that God will turn against us; He never will. His love is unconditional. The problem is that we have turned against Him, and in that state of mind we are violating all the necessary steps we must take to draw on Him as our divine Source of strength and help.

3. Joseph patiently waited for God to vindicate him and to honor both his faith and his positive attitudes. So should we! This must have been the most difficult thing Joseph had to do. Eleven years is a long time, and most of that time was spent in prison. Following the request he made to the cupbearer to remember him to Pharaoh, we're told that *another two years* went by before the cupbearer remembered what Joseph had done for him.

But that's getting ahead of our story. The important point at this juncture is that Joseph waited patiently for God to set the record straight.

The greatest temptation we all face when someone mistreats us is to seek revenge. Joseph had to face that temptation as well. But he overcame that temptation too. And in doing so, Joseph was not "overcome by evil." Rather he overcame "evil with good" (Rom. 12:21).

A MODERN-DAY JOSEPH

Is it possible to approach this kind of problem as Joseph did—to have the same attitudes? More than any other person, Corrie ten Boom stands out as a modern-day Joseph. She and her sister Betsie were placed in a Nazi concentration camp for hiding Jews in their home during the second world war. During a time of terrible mistreatment, Betsie died. Corrie's overall reaction to her predicament illustrates more powerfully Joseph's responses than anyone I know outside of Jesus Christ Himself. But she *was* human and she struggled desperately with forgiveness. One of her greatest tests came one day after she had been released. Listen to her own words as she describes this event:

It was in a church in Munich that I saw him—a balding, heavyset man in a gray overcoat, a brown felt hat clutched between his hands. People were filing out of the basement room where I had just spoken, moving along the rows of wooden chairs to the door at the rear. It was 1947 and I had come from Holland to defeated Germany with the message that God forgives.

It was the truth they needed most to hear in that bitter, bombed-out land, and I gave them my favorite mental picture. Maybe because the sea is never far from a Hollander's mind, I liked to think that that's where forgiven sins were thrown. "When we confess our sins," I said, "God casts them into the deepest ocean, gone forever. And even though I cannot find a Scripture for it, I believe God then places a sign out there that says, NO FISHING ALLOWED."

The solemn faces stared back at me, not quite daring to believe. There were never questions after a talk in Germany in 1947. People stood up in silence, in silence collected their wraps, in silence left the room.

And that's when I saw him, working his way forward against the others. One moment I saw the overcoat and the brown hat; the next, a blue uniform and a visored cap with its skull and crossbones. It came back with a rush: the huge room with its harsh overhead lights; the pathetic pile of dresses and shoes in the center of the floor; the shame of walking naked past this man. I could see my sister's frail form ahead of me, ribs sharp beneath the parchment skin. Betsie, how thin you were!

The place was Ravensbruck and the man who was making his way forward had been a guard—one of the most cruel guards.

Now he was in front of me, hand thrust out: "A fine message, Fraulein! How good it is to know that, as you say, all our sins are at the bottom of the sea!"

And I, who had spoken so glibly of forgiveness, fumbled in my pocketbook rather than take that hand. He would not remember me, of course—how could he remember one prisoner among those thousands of women?

But I remembered him and the leather crop swinging from his belt. I was face-to-face with one of my captors and my blood seemed to freeze.

"You mentioned Ravensbruck in your talk," he was saying. "I was a guard there." No, he did not remember me.

"But since that time," he went on, "I have become a Christian. I know that God has forgiven me for the cruel things I did there, but I would like to hear it from your lips as well. Fraulein,"—again the hand came out—"will you forgive me?"

And I stood there—I whose sins had again and

again been forgiven—and could not forgive. Betsie had died in that place—could he erase her slow terrible death simply for the asking?

It could not have been many seconds that he stood there—hand held out—but to me it seemed hours as I wrestled with the most difficult thing I had ever had to do.

For I had to do it—I knew that. The message that God forgives has a prior condition: that we forgive those who have injured us. "If you do not forgive men their trespasses," Jesus says, "neither will your Father in heaven forgive your trespasses."

I knew it not only as a commandment of God, but as a daily experience. Since the end of the war I had had a home in Holland for victims of Nazi brutality. Those who were able to forgive their former enemies were able also to return to the outside world and rebuild their lives, no matter what the physical scars. Those who nursed their bitterness remained invalids. It was as simple and as horrible as that.

And still I stood there with the coldness clutching my heart. But forgiveness is not an emotion—I knew that too. Forgiveness is an act of the will, and the will can function regardless of the temperature of the heart. "Jesus, help me!" I prayed silently. "I can lift my hand. I can do that much. You supply the feeling."

And so woodenly, mechanically, I thrust my hand into the one stretched out to me. And as I did, an incredible thing took place. The current started in my shoulder, raced down my arm, sprang into our joined hands. And then this healing warmth seemed to flood my whole being, bringing tears to my eyes.

"I forgive you, brother!" I cried. "With all my heart."

For a long moment we grasped each other's hands, the former guard and the former prisoner. I had never known God's love so intensely as I did then. But even so, I realized it was not my love. I had tried, and did not have the power. It was the power of the Holy Spirit as recorded in Romans 5:5, ". . . because the love of God is shed abroad in our hearts by the Holy Ghost which is given unto us."[2]

A PERSONAL CHALLENGE

1. Have I allowed bitterness to capture my soul because someone has treated me unjustly?

God says: "Get rid of all bitterness, rage and anger, brawling and slander, along with every form of malice. Be kind and compassionate to one another, forgiving each other, just as in Christ God forgave you" (Eph. 4:31,32).

2. Have I allowed my bitterness towards others to become bitterness towards God?

God says: "And we know that in all things God works for the good of those who love him, who have been called according to his purpose. . . . Who shall separate us from the love of Christ? Shall trouble or hardship or persecution or famine or nakedness or danger or sword?. . . No, in all these things we are more than conquerors through him who loved us" (Rom. 8:28,35,37).

3. Have I become vindictive towards those who have mistreated me, seeking to get even?

God says: "Do not repay anyone evil for evil. . . . Do not take revenge, my friends, but leave room for God's wrath, for it is written: 'It is mine to avenge; I will repay,' says the Lord. . . . Do not be overcome by evil, but overcome evil with good" (Rom. 12:17,19,21).

Notes

1. You can calculate Joseph's age at this juncture with two specific references. He was seventeen when Jacob made him his royal robe (Gen. 37:2). He was thirty when he became prime minister of Egypt (Gen. 41:46). And the events in chapter 40 took place two years before he became prime minister (Gen. 41:1).

2. Corrie ten Boom, *Tramp for the Lord* (Old Tappan, NJ: Fleming H. Revell Company, 1974), pp. 55-57.

6

Joseph's
Lesson in Waiting

GENESIS 40:23-41:40

- How has God used a "period of waiting" in your own life? What lessons did you learn?

- How did you handle this "period of waiting" emotionally?

- Is God allowing this process to happen in your life at the present time? If so, can you see some ultimate good that could result?

One of the greatest virtues a Christian needs, but which most of us lack to some degree or another, is patience—that capacity to maintain our spiritual and emotional equilibrium when things are happening within us and around us that make us uncomfortable.

Fortunately, we can usually alter our behavior and our circumstances sufficiently to eventually overcome most problems. However, there are occasions when it seems all we can do is wait! That is one of the most difficult situations we face in life, especially if we are unable to do something constructive to meet our personal needs and to reach our goals. In circumstances like these, we all *want* patience! But ironically, we want it *now*! ~~Sometimes we have no choice but to wait. It's out of our hands~~

One of the great virtues God was developing in Joseph's life was patience, which is the essence of learning to wait. And Joseph's greatest lessons in patience were learned during what must have been a very difficult but stretching time in his life.

JOSEPH'S TWO-YEAR WAIT
Genesis 40:23; 41:1

The last verse in chapter 40 of Genesis and the first verse in chapter 41 must be read together to experience the full impact of what must have happened in Joseph's heart and mind at this time. We read that "the chief cupbearer . . . *did not remember* Joseph; he *forgot him*." And the historical record continues—"When *two full years* had passed, Pharaoh had a dream" (Gen. 40:23,41:1).

Some Reflections on Joseph's Prison Experience

When Joseph interpreted the cupbearer's dream, reassuring him that he would be reinstated to his former position, he asked this high-ranking official to put in a good word for him to the king. This must have been Joseph's first ray of hope for release since his confinement to prison by Potiphar several years before. Joseph no doubt saw this opportunity as an answer to his prayers and a reward for waiting so long. After all, he had not allowed bitterness to grip his soul, and he had fulfilled his duties faithfully without complaining. Every day he must have waited for some word, for some indication that Pharaoh was concerned about his plight. After all, if the cupbearer had told the whole story, Pharaoh would have known that Joseph's God had enabled him to interpret dreams accurately. Had not the cupbearer been restored in three days and the baker executed just as Joseph prophesied? Surely Pharaoh would be interested in discovering more about Joseph's ability, for it was not something new for the king to consult magicians and wisemen who could predict the future.

But no word came. Days turned into weeks and weeks into months and months into *"two full years"*! What hope he had must have faded. We must remember that God had *not* revealed to Joseph what was going to happen. The fact that the Lord gave him the ability to predict someone else's future did not mean that he had a supernatural ability to predict his own. Joseph had to continue his prison experience by faith, continuing to hope that God would make it possible for him to be released.

Some Reflections on Joseph's Family Experience

Why did Joseph want to be free? It was not only that he was innocent. More than anything he wanted to return to his family in Canaan. He made this clear to the cupbearer, at least by implication, when he said, "I was forcibly carried off from the land of the Hebrews" (Gen. 40:15). In other words, he was saying, "I don't really belong here. I was brought here against my will. I want to go home."

Let's think for a moment about Joseph's family relationships. It had been eleven long years since he had seen his father, the man he had been so close to. He was Jacob's favorite son. And Joseph's last visual memory of his father was when Jacob had so naively sent him, clothed in his royal robe, to check on his brothers in Shechem.

Furthermore, since Joseph was such a sensitive man, he must have grieved deeply for his father who had believed that Joseph was devoured by a wild animal. Think how often he must have wanted to, somehow and in some way, send a message to his father that he was still alive. Better yet, how wonderful it would be to make a sudden appearance and surprise his father—that is, if he were still alive, another thought that must have obsessed his heart and mind. Joseph longed to go home.

Homesickness is real no matter what our age. I remember when I was a young boy I was away from my family for *two whole weeks*. It was my first experience in being away from home for any period of time. I was visiting one of my favorite uncles. One evening at the end of the first week, I was attending a special prayer service in another home. While the people were singing and praying, the most awful feeling came over me. I began to weep, first softly and then uncontrollably. No matter what I did to try to stop, I couldn't. For at least an hour, I really didn't understand what was happening, and neither did the other folks in the room. I think some of them thought I was under conviction! In retrospect, I now know I was a victim of homesickness. I missed my family so desperately I thought I was going to die. And remember it was *only two weeks*—not *two* years or *thirteen* as with Joseph.

I also remember the long summers I spent a thousand miles away from my wife and children when I was doing graduate work at New York University. Though I was very busy with my studies, I dreaded weekends. There I was in the middle of New York City with people everywhere; however, I felt like the loneliest man on earth. I missed my family terribly. Incidently, at that time I must have been about the same age as Joseph at this point in his life. But fortunately I was still in my native homeland. I could write and receive letters. I could use the telephone. There were other Christians with whom to fellowship.

Even so, I was still lonely. Think for a moment how Joseph must have felt. He was completely shut away from his family for years with no opportunity to communicate, and humanly speaking, no forseeable opportunity for freedom, either to move about freely in Egypt or to return home!

Those days of waiting after Joseph's encounter with the

cupbearer must have initially brought him hope. And then it began to fade, leaving him more emotionally distraught than ever. But fortunately, Joseph had hope beyond hope. That's what kept him from despair all during this terrible ordeal. His hope was ultimately in God, not in Potiphar, not in the cupbearer, not even in the king of Egypt. When men failed him he knew God was still with him, even in prison. This is what enabled him to endure in the midst of deep sorrow and distress.

PHARAOH'S DREAMS AND JOSEPH'S INTERPRETATION
Genesis 41:1-32

Dreams played a very important part in Joseph's life. Many years before it was his own dreams that made his brothers so jealous and angry. It was those dreams that got him into trouble in the first place. And now, years later, it was his God-given ability to interpret dreams that would be a means for his release from prison and a promotion in Egypt that would affect not only his destiny but the destiny of the Egyptians, the destiny of his own family; and the destiny of the great nation of Israel that would eventually evolve.

The Dreams (Gen. 41:2-8)

"Two *full* years" after the cupbearer had been reinstated—probably again on Pharaoh's birthday—the king had a dream. He saw seven well-fed cows grazing in the Nile River. Then he saw seven undernourished cows come up out of the Nile. They immediately devoured the seven well-fed cows (Gen. 41:1-4).

Chances are Pharaoh wasn't too puzzled about this first dream. However, he had a second dream. This time seven healthy heads of grain were devoured by seven "thin and scorched" heads of grain (Gen. 41:5-7). When Pharaoh awakened after this second dream he was indeed "troubled." He immediately saw the similarities in the two dreams. In both dreams there was a set of sevens followed by a second set of sevens. The first set of sevens involved *prosperity* and the second set of sevens involved the *lack of prosperity*. Furthermore, in both dreams the second set of sevens that *lacked prosperity* devoured the first set of sevens that were *prosperous*. If Pharaoh had reflected carefully, which he must have done, he would have noticed that the one dream involved a *pastoral* setting and the second an *agricultural* setting. As Edersheim puts it, one dream involved the *flocks* of Egypt and the second the *crops* of Egypt. Together, these two aspects of the Egyptian economy represented the lifeblood of the land and its people.

No wonder Pharaoh was troubled! Like the dreams Joseph had interpreted for the chief cupbearer and baker two years before, these dreams represented more than bizarre, subconscious thinking. And Pharaoh sensed it so much so that "he sent for all the magicians and wise men of Egypt." One after another he told each one his dreams, but "no one could interpret them" (Gen. 41:8). I'm sure they tried desperately to discover a satisfactory meaning, but the king knew that they did not have the answers to his questions.

The Cupbearer Remembers (Gen. 41:9-13)

Observing what was probably a rather long and involved process—perhaps taking weeks—was none other than the chief cupbearer who had been restored to his position two years before. Day after day he watched all the magicians and wise men of Egypt come and go, leaving the king more troubled and frustrated each time. And then, at some point in time, he remembered his own experience with Joseph! Or perhaps he gained enough courage to talk about what he had forced himself to forget. Whatever his thoughts, he came to Pharaoh and said, "Today I am reminded of my shortcomings" (Gen. 41:9). He recounted the time he spent in prison as a result of Pharaoh's anger. He also told the king about this "young Hebrew" who was there (he probably had forgotten his name) who was a servant of Potiphar. "We told him our dreams," the cupbearer continued, "and he interpreted them for us, giving each man the interpretation of his dream" (Gen. 41:12). Of course the thing that impressed Pharaoh the most was that "things turned out exactly" as Joseph had interpreted them (Gen. 41:13).

Pharaoh *was* impressed! He immediately "sent for Joseph" (Gen. 41:14), who was released from the dungeon and given opportunity to shave and change his clothes. He then appeared before Pharaoh.

The Interpretation (Gen. 41:14-32)

Pharaoh related to Joseph that he had no one who could interpret his dreams. "But," he said, "I have heard it said of you that when you hear a dream you can interpret it" (Gen. 41:15).

Joseph's response was magnificent. How easy it would have been to try to impress Pharaoh with his own abilities. This was his big opportunity! He was standing before the *king of Egypt*! If he could prove himself to Pharaoh he might be released from prison.

But Joseph took absolutely no credit. " 'I cannot do it,' Joseph replied to Pharaoh, 'but God will give Pharaoh the answer he desires' " (Gen. 41:16).

We can now see even more clearly why both Potiphar and the prison warden were impressed with Joseph's abilities, and why they saw a direct connection between the God he worshiped and the success he enjoyed. All along, Joseph had given the Lord credit.

Pharaoh was now impressed more than ever. He related his two dreams to Joseph (Gen. 41:17-24). And just as he had done two years before, Joseph was able to give an instant interpretation. There were no incantations, no religious exercises, no pagan practices—as the magicians would have done. He simply and succinctly told Pharaoh the meaning of both dreams. "The dreams of Pharaoh are one and the same." Furthermore, Joseph said, "God has revealed to Pharaoh what he is about to do" (Gen. 41:25). In short, Joseph told Pharaoh that the first sets of seven referred to "seven years of great abundance" and the second sets of seven referred to "seven years of famine." And to make sure Pharaoh really understood the seriousness of the prediction, Joseph told him that "the reason the dream was given . . . in two forms" was so that Pharaoh would know that what was going to happen had been "firmly decided by God" and that it would happen "soon" (Gen. 41:32).

Pharaoh's heart had already been prepared for Joseph's interpretation. In fact, he had already concluded that his two dreams were in reality only one (Gen. 41:15). Perhaps he had correlated this much from his own reflections on his dreams, or his wise men may have pointed out this obvious similarity. But now *all* the pieces fell into place in his mind. Furthermore, Pharaoh would have done some very careful research on Joseph before he even brought him into his presence. He obviously knew of Joseph's success and responsibility, both in Potiphar's house as well as in prison. Pharaoh was aware that he was not dealing with just an ordinary young man. *All of Joseph's faithful efforts and his positive attitudes over the last thirteen years were now paying significant dividends.*

JOSEPH'S PROPOSAL AND PROMOTION
Genesis 41:33-40

Joseph was wise enough to also see unfolding before him a plan that God had designed all along. He knew that Pharaoh was listening intently and was open to suggestions. And at this juncture he made a very wise proposal. He suggested to Pharaoh that he "look for a discerning and wise

He was not so mad at God that his eyes were blinded.

man"—a man he could put "in charge of the land of Egypt." He further suggested a plan for storing up food "during the seven years of abundance," which in turn could be used and distributed "during the seven years of famine" (Gen. 41:33-36).

Pharaoh's response to Joseph's plan was positive. Not only was he impressed with the proposal, but in Pharaoh's mind he *knew* who the man should be. It was none other than Joseph. Turning to his officials, he asked, "Can we find anyone like this man, one in whom is the spirit of God?" (Gen. 41:38). Pharaoh knew that Joseph's capabilities were supernatural. Furthermore, he now saw him against the backdrop of *all the other* magicians and wise men of Egypt. Joseph stood head and shoulders above them all!

Think for a moment what God had allowed to happen. Had Joseph come before Pharaoh two years before, chances are it would have been only because of the king's curiosity. There would have been no personal need or sense of urgency in his own heart. He would not have called for all the wise men of Egypt. Consequently, there would have been no opportunity for Pharaoh to compare *Joseph's success* with *their failure*. The thoroughness with which Pharaoh tried to determine the meaning of his dreams is seen in his conclusion: *"There is no one so discerning and wise as you"* (Gen. 41:39).

The *extent* of Pharaoh's trust is clear from the *extent* of Joseph's promotion. He went from "prison" to "palace"— not only to live there, but to have authority over the whole kingdom of Egypt. Thus Pharaoh said, "Only with respect to the throne will I be greater than you" (Gen. 41:40).

SOME PERSONAL REFLECTIONS

1. Learning to wait patiently strengthens our confidence in God without reducing the self-confidence we need to function in life. Joseph did not lack self-confidence. If

anything, at age seventeen, he probably had too much. Or
perhaps more accurately, he had not balanced it properly
with confidence in God. If he had, he would have been
more cautious in how he shared his dreams with his family.

However, through all of Joseph's difficulties there is no
evidence that he ever lost his *self*-confidence. Conversely,
there is significant evidence that he developed his *God*-con-
fidence.

How clear this is when he emerged from prison to stand
before Pharaoh. Had he lacked self-confidence on the one
hand, or had he been over-confident on the other, he would
have tried to impress Pharaoh with his own abilities. But
Joseph's response was in essence, *"I* cannot do it, but *God*
can." It's evident that Joseph believed this to be true now
more than ever before. True, he had believed it two years
earlier when he first met the king's cupbearer and baker
(Gen. 40:6). But two years of waiting had only convinced
Joseph even more.

Men and women of God who are forced to live in circumstances that are totally beyond their control emerge
more convinced than ever before that without God, they can
do nothing. Their faith, though "refined by fire" comes
forth like gold. It's "proved genuine" (1 Pet. 1:7).

2. A period of waiting often allows time for true character to be developed *and* revealed. Again, how true in
Joseph's life. Though he must have wavered often, he never
turned away from God. He weathered every storm. Though
tempted to be bitter, immoral and proud—he never let down
his guard. How else could these qualities have been developed and revealed?

And how true in a Christian's life! There are things we
cannot learn apart from a period of waiting, and often that
period must be in a context of adversity.

3. A period of waiting often creates opportunities for
advancement that may not happen otherwise. What if
Joseph *had* gone before Pharaoh two years before? The king

Eg Karate injury 2 yrs out

would have had no opportunity to compare Joseph's abilities or his character with that of the wisest men in all of Egypt. God's timing was perfect in Joseph's life. And because it was, Joseph was not only released from prison but promoted by Pharaoh to the highest position in the kingdom.

And this principle may be true in our own lives. Though our opportunities may be far more limited in scope, they will be there. Our temptation is to get in a hurry—especially if everything is not going our way. Perhaps God is saying, "Wait, and if you do, what I have for you will be far greater than anything you can create for yourself!"

This principle of course is not an excuse for inactivity, laziness or indecisiveness. Joseph never rationalized his circumstances. In fact, his self-confidence and inner motivation were very obvious when he suggested to the king that he needed a wise man to oversee the Egyptian economy, knowing full well that the king would probably conclude that he, Joseph, was that man. But he took that step only when he knew in his heart that God's red light had turned to green.

CORRIE SPEAKS AGAIN

In her book *Tramp for the Lord,* Corrie ten Boom describes her feelings the day she was miraculously released from a Nazi concentration camp. In many respects, she and Joseph had a lot in common:

When you are dying—when you stand at the gate of eternity—you see things from a different perspective than when you think you may live for a long time. I had been standing at that gate for many months, living in Barracks 28 in the shadow of the crematorium. Every time I saw the smoke pouring from the hideous smokestacks I knew it was the last remains of some poor woman who had been with me in Ravensbruck.

Often I asked myself, "When will it be my time to be killed or die?"

But I was not afraid. Following Betsie's death, God's Presence was even more real. Even though I was looking into the valley of the shadow of death, I was not afraid. It is here that Jesus comes the closest; taking our hand, and leading us through.

One week before the order came to kill all the women of my age, I was free. I still do not understand all the details of my release from Ravensbruck. All I know is, it was a miracle of God.

I stood in the prison yard—waiting the final order. Beyond the walls with their strands of barbed wire stood the silent trees of the German forest, looking so much like the gray-green sets on the back of one of our theater stages in Holland.

Mimi, one of the fellow prisoners, came within whispering distance. "Tiny died this morning," she said without looking at me. "And Marie also."

Tiny! "Oh, Lord, thank You for letting me point her to Jesus who has now ushered her safely into Your Presence." And Marie. I knew her well. She lived in my barracks and had attended my Bible talks. Like Tiny, Marie had also accepted Jesus as her Lord. I looked back at the long rows of barracks. "Lord, if it was only for Tiny and Marie—that they might come to know you before they died—then it was all worthwhile."

A guard spoke harshly, telling Mimi to leave the yard. Then he said to me, "Face the gate. Do not turn around."

The gate swung open and I glimpsed the lake in front of the camp. I could smell freedom.

"Follow me," a young girl in an officer's uniform said to me. I walked slowly through the gate, never looking back. Behind me I heard the hinges squeak as the gate swung shut. I was free, and flooding through my mind were the words of Jesus to the church at Philadelphia: Behold, I have set before thee an open door, and no man can shut it . . . (Revelation 3:8)[1]

A PERSONAL CHALLENGE

Today, right now, you may be facing a difficult period in your own life—a period of anxious waiting. Have you asked yourself the following questions?

1. How can I use this experience to develop my confidence and faith in God?

God says: "Consider it pure joy, my brothers, whenever you face trials of many kinds, because you know that the testing of your faith develops perseverance. Perseverance must finish its work so that you may be mature and complete, not lacking in anything" (Jas. 1:2-4).

2. Is God using this experience to develop and reveal my character?

God says: "Not only so, but we also rejoice in our sufferings, because we know that suffering produces perseverance; perseverance, character; and character, hope" (Rom. 5:3,4).

3. Is God using this experience to provide an opportunity to use me sometime in the future far more than He could at the present time?

God says: "And we know that in all things God works for the good of those who love him, who have been called according to his purpose" (Rom. 8:28).

Note
1. Corrie Ten Boom, *Tramp for the Lord* (Old Tappan, NJ: Fleming H. Revell Company, 1974), pp. 23,24.

7

Joseph's
Preparation in Perspective

GENESIS 41:41-57

• How is God preparing you to avoid prideful behavior?

• How is God preparing you to persevere when you face difficult circumstances?

• How is God preparing you to perform well as you face more and more responsibility?

Most of us have come to some point where we can look back on life's journey and gradually, or perhaps somewhat suddenly, see a very distinct mosaic that we have not seen before. Joseph reached that point in his life when Pharaoh promoted him to serve as prime minister of Egypt. In a sense this is the theme of this whole story. Joseph may have caught glimpses of some supernatural meaning in his very difficult and painful thirteen-year experience. But God's divine pattern for his life must have come into focus rather suddenly when he was promoted so quickly and so dramatically. Seldom does any person released from prison, who is a foreigner, even when innocent, suddenly become a primary ruler of one of the most significant and affluent kingdoms in the world.

FROM PRISON TO PALACE
Genesis 41:41-45

Once Pharaoh learned of Joseph's supernatural ability to interpret dreams and discovered the management skills he had demonstrated so faithfully both in Potiphar's house and in prison, he wasted no time in releasing him and promoting him to a very lofty and responsible position in Egypt. "I hereby put you *in charge* of the whole land of Egypt," he said to Joseph (Gen. 41:41).

To be put "in charge" of something was not a new concept or experience in Joseph's life story. Potiphar had "put him *in charge* of his household" (Gen. 39:4). The warden had "put Joseph *in charge* of all those held in the prison" (Gen. 39:22). And now Pharaoh put him "*in charge* of the whole land of Egypt" (Gen. 41:41). And in each instance the man involved had observed not only Joseph's positive attitudes and unique abilities, but that his success was directly related to God's blessing on his life and work.

Joseph's promotion at this point in his life is mind-boggling and almost breathtaking. One day he was a restricted Hebrew slave serving an open-ended prison sentence. The next day he was in Pharaoh's court, interpreting his dreams, giving him wisdom and advice; then he was assigned to the highest position in the Egyptian government outside of being the king himself.

The privileges, power, and prestige that went with this promotion accentuate why this event is so dramatic and incredible, and indeed a miracle of God.

He had geographical control. He was responsible for "the *whole* land of Egypt"—a nation in ancient history comparable in influence and size only to the Babylonian Empire. Egypt's wealth was limitless.

He had financial authority. "Pharaoh took his *signet* ring . . . and put it on Joseph's finger" (Gen. 41:42). This gave Joseph an open-ended budget. With the king's ring he could stamp any invoice, authorize any expenditure, and pay any amount to carry out the king's business.

He had social prestige. Pharaoh dressed Joseph in royal garments. He provided him with a kingly wardrobe, and each robe was made of "fine linen"—the most exquisite fabric in all of Egypt. Furthermore, he "put a gold chain around his neck" (Gen. 41:42). Though we're not told its size or value, we can safely conclude that its shape and price were commensurate with Joseph's new position.

He had royal privileges. Pharaoh provided Joseph with his own private chariot—comparable to a presidential limousine in our culture today. His "license plate" read "2"! Being "second-in-command," he—like the king—was assigned a group of men who rode ahead of him and cleared the way (Gen. 41:43). Like any high government official, he had his own security force. In addition, these men made sure these people honored Joseph's presence, insisting that they "bow the knee" before him (*KJV*).

He had political power. Joseph's greatest honor came when Pharaoh informed him that as king, he himself would not even make a decision regarding Egyptian affairs without Joseph's advice and approval. "I am Pharaoh," he said, "but without your word, no one will lift hand or foot in all Egypt" (Gen. 41:44). That, of course, represents the ultimate in political and economic authority. In that sense, Joseph became one of the most esteemed, most respected and most powerful men in the world of his day.

He had religious position. There are two final things mentioned in the biblical text that happened to Joseph when he was promoted. First, Pharaoh changed his name, and then he gave him a wife. His new name was Zaphe*nath-*

Paneah (Gen. 41:45). Inherent in this name—the little word *nath*—is the idea that "God speaks and lives." Though in the minds of Egyptian priests this referred to one of their gods, it really represents Pharaoh's best attempt at indicating that he believed and wanted others to believe that Joseph was no ordinary man. In his own pagan way it seems he was trying to acknowledge Joseph's God who had helped him interpret his dreams. In the religious life in Egypt, there was always room for another god.

Joseph's wife was "Ase*nath* daughter of Potiphera, priest of On" (Gen. 41:45). This man's full identity and position in Egypt is unknown. However, it is clear he was involved in the religious system, and that his daughter's name included the same idea as Joseph's new name. Again, *nath* (Ase*nath*) means "God speaks and lives." Together this couple not only represented the king of Egypt but deity as well. And their names would constantly remind people of that fact.

GOD'S SPECIAL PREPARATION
Genesis 41:46

One of the most significant facts in this whole chapter is mentioned in verse 46. When Pharaoh gave Joseph this high position, he was only "thirty years old." Few men have been given this kind of power and authority at so young an age. And when they are, it frequently leads to arrogance, irresponsible behavior and often their downfall. There are some exceptions of course—and Joseph was one of those exceptions.

But this leads us to some very important observations. The crazy-quilt pattern to this point in Joseph's life now began to take on meaning. Joseph's bizarre experiences suddenly turned into a beautiful tapestry in his heart and mind as memories, both pleasant and painful, flooded his soul. The last thirteen years of his life began to make sense.

There was now rhyme and reason. And what was often very painful during those years faded in his memory as he now understood God's purpose in allowing him to experience so much unjust treatment (Gen. 41:51).

How had God prepared Joseph for his unique position in Egypt? What was God teaching him? The lessons he was learning can be focused in at least three important areas—*pride, perseverance* and *performance.*

1. *First, God was preparing Joseph to be on guard against prideful behavior.* J. Oswald Sanders once wrote, "Not every man can carry a full cup. Sudden elevation frequently leads to pride and a fall. The most exacting test of all to survive is prosperity."

Since we know the overall story of Joseph's story, we also know he handled a "full cup" very well—in spite of his youthfulness. And his "sudden elevation" to power did not lead to pride and a fall, but to even greater success and spirituality. He not only survived this test of prosperity but used it for the honor and glory of God.

This is, of course, a tribute to Joseph. But more so, it points to what God had done in his life. The Lord had prepared Joseph well for this position. Thirteen years of very difficult experiences marked his life. He would never forget the pit from which he came to Potiphar's house, or the prison that was his home for most of those years before he became the king's prime minister.

Remember too that Joseph was a prime candidate for pride. He was a favorite son. He had been given a special place in his family at a very early age, even though he had ten brothers *older* than he. His father had given him a richly ornamented robe, signifying to all his special place. And at the tender age of seventeen God had allowed him to have two dreams that verified his special place in the family and in God's scheme of things (Gen. 37:5-10). And later we are told specifically that Joseph was a "well-built and handsome young man." And certainly, without doubt, his performance both at home and in Egypt indicated that he was very intelligent.

Joseph was one of those men who had everything going for him. He was *indeed* a prime candidate for pride. But it was all of these privileges and qualities that would some day contribute to his success in Egypt, but *not* until he was "refined by fire" and "brought forth as gold" (1 Pet. 1:7); not until he was prepared to handle the prestige and power that God designed for him.

God had great plans for Joseph. And the Lord knew he would rise to the occasion only after and when severely tested. And all along the way Joseph passed each test satisfactorily. He did not become bitter. He had a forgiving spirit. He maintained a servant's heart. His self-confidence became properly balanced with God-confidence. And most of all, he never forgot the grace of God in sustaining him in his most trying years! All of these factors were being woven into the fabric of his personality to help him guard against pride when suddenly elevated to his position in Egypt.

2. *Second, God was preparing Joseph to persevere in some very difficult and demanding circumstances.* There's a price tag on every high-level leadership position. There will be those who will become jealous. There will be rumors and false accusations. There will be misunderstandings and breakdowns in communication. By the very nature of the position, leaders must take responsibility for the mistakes of others. There will be sleepless nights and problems that can never be completely solved. There will be more to do than can be done. And unless prepared for these pressures, no man or woman will persevere.

Joseph faced all of these problems. His responsibility was enormous. And perhaps his greatest stress came from the unconditional trust Pharaoh placed in him—and in his God! Joseph was under pressure to *not* fail his human master *or* his divine Master.

Fortunately, Joseph's preparation was also spiritual.

With every difficulty, Joseph grew in his relationship with God. He learned to trust God. He saw God work on his behalf. Joseph knew the Lord would help him fulfill his task in Egypt—enormous as it was. He had learned this through thirteen years of very excruciating but highly profitable experience! Without it he would not have been ready to handle the economic affairs of Egypt.

3. *Third, God was preparing Joseph to perform well when given a very demanding task.*

JOSEPH'S PLAN IN ACTION
Genesis 41:47-57

The rest of chapter 41 spells out the seven years of plenty in Egypt and the beginning of the seven years of famine. Joseph's task called for superhuman wisdom and strength, especially for a young man in his thirties. Joseph supervised throughout Egypt a gigantic storehouse operation. In every city he "stored up huge quantities of grain, like the sand of the sea." In fact, the surplus became so great "he stopped keeping records because it was beyond measure" (Gen. 41:49).

When the predicted famine hit, Joseph then faced the mammoth job of distribution. Maintaining equality would in itself be an unbelievable task. The full force of managing this operation lay squarely on Joseph's shoulders. When people began to come to the king for food, he "told all the Egyptians, 'Go to Joseph and do what he tells you' " (Gen. 41:55).

But the famine affected more than Egypt. It spread throughout the world. Joseph administered the distribution of food not only among the people of Egypt, but among those who came from other countries to buy food (Gen. 41:56,57). And this factor introduces us to the most exciting part of Joseph's life story. God allowed him to be sold into Egypt, not only to bear His name among these pagan people but to be part of the future destiny of his own family and God's chosen people, the nation of Israel.

But at this point it is clear that, at age thirty, Joseph could *never* have handled this "world task" without an intensive and experience-oriented course in management. It began in Potiphar's house, where he managed his whole household. And it continued in prison where he was eventually responsible for all the prisoners. And thirteen years later, he was "put . . . in charge of the whole land of Egypt" (Gen. 41:41).

God's plan for Joseph was on schedule. His preparation was tailor-made for the task God had for him. And because Joseph passed each test, learned from each experience, and learned to trust God more, he was ready when God opened the door of opportunity. He handled prestige and power without succumbing to pride. He persevered with patience. And he performed his duties faithfully and successfully. He was prepared.

SOME PERSONAL REFLECTIONS

What God taught Joseph He wants to teach every one of us. True, few if any of us will ever be assigned a heavy task like Joseph. And fortunately, few of us will need the experiences Joseph needed to prepare us for our tasks! But we all need to learn the same things he did, no matter what our responsibilities and position in life.

1. If we'll let Him, God will teach us lessons that will help avoid the pitfall of *pride*. We all face this temptation. Joseph certainly did. And we all fail at times. But God cannot and will not use a Christian to the full who is prideful. In the book of Proverbs we read that "there are six things the Lord hates, seven that are detestable to him." He lists them as follows: "*Haughty eyes,* a lying tongue, hands that shed innocent blood, a heart that devises wicked schemes, feet that are quick to rush into evil, a false witness who pours out lies and a man who stirs up dissension among brothers" (Prov. 6:16-19).

At the top of the list is *pride*. This sin has destroyed the effectiveness of more Christians than any other and has kept many from rising to the level of responsibility God had in mind. But, if we will let Him, He'll prepare us!

Samuel Rutherford once stated that we should "praise God for the hammer, the file and the furnace." He went on to explain that the "hammer molds us, the file shapes us and the fire tempers us." All three experiences of course are painful, but we can praise God for them because we know and love the God who wields them.

A. W. Tozer, commenting on Rutherford's statement, wrote, "The devil, things and people being what they are, it is necessary to use the hammer, the file and the furnace in the holy work of preparing the saint for the sainthood. It is doubtful whether God can bless a man greatly until he has hurt him deeply."[1]

It must be emphasized however that God allows hurt in His children's lives only in order to help them. In Joseph's life, all of the pain and humiliation that came his way would some day help him to face the temptation towards pride and be victorious! Only a man prepared as Joseph was prepared could have avoided falling prey to pride when suddenly given such awesome position and power.

2. If we'll let Him, God will prepare us both spiritually and emotionally to *persevere* as we face difficult responsibilities. I remember an experience in my own life that I *now* see as God's preparation. When I graduated from Moody Bible Institute I was involved in a ministry I considered a great privilege. But during this experience I became very disappointed with several key Christian leaders. For several long months I entered a very dark period in my life. I began to doubt my own salvation. I even wondered if there was a God. At times I was so miserable and disillusioned I was tempted to leave the ministry completely.

At the time I did not realize God allowed this experience to deal with some serious spiritual and emotional areas in my own life. When I left that ministry and began graduate work near Chicago, I was suddenly given an opportunity to join the Moody Bible Institute faculty. At the time I was only twenty-three years old. I began to see that previous difficulties had a purpose. God was allowing me to get prepared for this unique teaching opportunity to prepare other young people for Christian service. Without those dark days, learning to persevere through some very difficult circumstances, I don't believe I would have been able to endure and survive the tasks God opened for me.

In retrospect I believe God gave me a choice during that difficult period. I could have left the ministry as I was tempted to do. If I had, I may never have gone on to the next level of opportunity in God's service. It may have changed the whole direction of my life.

And at various points along the way, God gives all of us certain choices. We can either persevere in the midst of difficulties and learn valuable lessons about ourselves and what it takes to persevere in even more demanding and stretching responsibilities in doing the will of God, or we can choose to turn away and take what appears at the moment to be an easier way. In some instances we may even turn aside from His perfect will.

As no other teacher, God knows exactly what curriculum we *each* need to both prepare us in specific areas of our personality and to also prepare us for specific tasks. And if we pass each test along the way, He will advance us to another level in His great work on earth. On the other hand, if we want to settle for less, He will usually not violate our will.

3. If we let Him, God will design a curriculum to prepare us to *perform well* when given greater and greater responsibility. With advancement, of course, comes greater pressure and the need for greater skills. But with greater pressure also comes personal growth and more meaningful and lasting fruit in the kingdom of God—now and eternally.

There is nothing more important in life than to do the will of God and to advance His work. Our comfort must always be a secondary consideration. After all, the Lord never promised us a rose garden on this earth. In fact, Jesus said, "Take up my cross and follow me." There are of course marvelous rewards. There is nothing more satisfying than to point people to Jesus Christ and to know we are honoring Him in what we do. But there are times we must pass through the valley to reach the next level in God's plan for our lives.

PERSONAL CHALLENGE

Think for a moment about the mosaic in your life. As you reflect, can you see meaning in your past and present experiences? What is God doing to prepare you, to equip you, to conform you into His image? Fortunately we have Joseph's experience to guide us, and the whole of Scripture. Even in the midst of darkness, we can see light because we know God loves us, that He will never forsake us and that, if we trust Him, we will "come forth as gold." Will you let Him guide and control your life?

One of my most enjoyable experiences is to drive over a mountain pass that consists of dozens of switchbacks. One of my favorites is Cook City Highway in Montana. When I lived for two years in Billings a number of years ago, I must have driven over this pass a dozen times. Climbing up through the mountain town of Big Timber, you finally reach an 11,000-foot summit and then descend the other side, eventually ending up in Yellowstone National Park.

As you ascend the pass, you can periodically pull off the highway, stop, and look back. There, winding down the mountain and into the valley below, is a series of switchbacks. While climbing, all you can see is the road a few yards ahead and behind. But as you reach each lookout, you can see the panorama and pattern below. In some instances you can see every switchback.

Finally you reach the summit, and both behind and ahead you can see where you have come from and where you are going. You can see the big picture.

When Joseph was promoted to prime minister in Egypt, he in a sense had reached the summit in God's plan for his life. Now both the past and the future made sense. Though many details in his future were still invisible and uncertain, God's overall mosaic was clear.

Can you believe that God will some day do the same for you? He will—if you let Him!

1. You must acknowledge your sin that separates you and all mankind from God.

God says, "For all have sinned and fall short of the glory of God" (Rom. 3:23).
"For the wages of sin is death . . ." (Rom. 6:23).

2. You must realize and understand that Jesus Christ paid the penalty for your sins and the sins of the whole world when He died on the cross.

God says, "But God demonstrates his own love for us in this: While we were still sinners, Christ died for us" (Rom. 5:8).
"For God so loved the world that he gave his one and only Son, that whosoever believes in him shall not perish but have eternal life" (John 3:16).

3. You must receive Jesus Christ as your own personal Saviour from sin.

God says, "Yet to all who received him, to those who believed in his name, he gave the right to become children of God" (John 1:12).

"For it is by grace you have been saved, through faith—and this not from yourselves, it is the gift of God—not by works, so that no one can boast" (Eph. 2:8,9).

4. You must make Jesus Christ Lord of your life. This means obeying His Word and trusting Him day by day in all circumstances.

God says, "Trust in the Lord with all your heart and lean not on your own understanding; in all your ways acknowledge him, and he will make your paths straight" (Prov. 3:5,6).

Note
1. Aiden W. Tozer, *Root of the Righteous* (Harrisburg, PA: Christian Publications, Inc., nd), p. 137.

8

Joseph's
Healing Experience

GENESIS 41:50-52

- Over the years, what has caused the most emotional pain in your life?

- On the other hand, what has God used to bring the most emotional healing in your life?

There is no way any human being can endure what Joseph went through for thirteen years without experiencing negative after-effects, particularly at the emotional level. And Joseph *was* human, just like any one of us. Though he had a very unique relationship with God he was not exempt from the same fears and anxieties we all experience when we are rejected by those we love, when we are falsely accused by those we are loyal to, when we are punished for the sins and mistakes of others, and when we are willfully forgotten by those we have helped the most. Because of these painful experiences, Joseph suffered deeply.

But God did not forget or forsake Joseph, either during those dark days or afterwards. Though he must have often wondered whether God really cared, Joseph never turned away from God. And once his days of testing and captivity came to an end, he began to experience God's healing balm in his soul.

How did God bring this mental and emotional healing to Joseph's heart and mind? The answer is tucked away in three power-packed verses in chapter 41. Though very clear and to the point, it's easy to overlook and miss the great lessons that emerge from these three verses.

After Joseph's promotion and "before the years of famine came," we're told that his wife Asenath gave birth to two sons (Gen. 41:50). The names Joseph gave these two boys, along with his personal explanation as to why he named them Manasseh and Ephraim, are significant clues to understand *how* God brought healing to Joseph's inner being. Furthermore, God still uses this method today, no matter what the cause of our suffering.

MANASSEH—"GOD HAS MADE ME FORGET"
Genesis 41:51

Joseph named his first son *Manasseh,* literally meaning "one who causes to forget." He then explained why he chose this name. "It is because God has made me *forget* all my trouble and all my father's household" (Gen. 41:51). The connection is clear. There is a very definite cause-effect relationship between Manasseh's birth and Joseph's ability to *forget* his painful past.

What Did Joseph Actually "Forget"?

Did he forget the traumatic experience when he was rejected by his brothers? Did he forget that day when they stripped him of his richly ornamented robe and threw him into a pit? Did he forget the argument his brothers had regarding whether or not to take his life? Did he forget that horrible moment when they bartered with the Midianite merchants and finally settled on his price as a slave—twenty shekels of silver? Did he forget those days as he trudged wearily over the desert roads bound for a strange land, leaving his family far behind? Did he forget the slave block in Egypt where he was auctioned off to the highest bidder? Did he forget the daily experience of being exposed to sexual temptations by a very seductive and sensuous woman? Did he forget her cries of "rape, rape" when he ran away, refusing to violate his moral principles and his master's trust? Did he forget those long years in prison as an innocent man? Did he forget the cupbearer's failure to remember him when he was restored to Potiphar's right hand? DId he forget those lonely hours thinking about his father and his deceased mother? Did he forget his little brother Benjamin, who was only a young lad when Joseph was taken into captivity?

The answer to all of these questions must be no. Joseph never forgot any of these events. The details were indelibly etched in his memory. If he had forgotten, the overall experience would have been of little value. Furthermore, he wouldn't have mentioned in these verses his "trouble" and his "father's household" when Manasseh was born. In fact, he would have no doubt chosen a different name for his firstborn if he had forgotten altogether.

What, then, did God enable Joseph to forget? It was the *pain* associated with those events. The emotional sting was gone. He was not in bondage to past experiences. There was no lingering bitterness, no inhibiting fear, no debilitating emotional sensitivity, and no obsessive thoughts that plagued his mind, or compulsive behavior that dominated his actions. Joseph had no regrets. God had healed his memories.

What Means Did God Use to Bring About Emotional Healing?

If you think about this question for a moment, the answer is clear. First, God gave Joseph a wife—another human being to fill the void in his life and to help him forget his loneliness. We know little of Asenath, but we can conclude that she was a very special lady. It would be difficult to imagine that after so many difficulties and heartaches God would allow Joseph to marry a woman who would make his life even more miserable. If that had happened, he would never have experienced emotional healing. And if he had not experienced emotional healing, he would never have been able to handle the superhuman task of directing the economic affairs of Egypt. All of his energy would have been diverted to trying to resolve his domestic problems.

And that of course can happen to any husband. In Proverbs we read that it is "better to live in a desert than with a quarrelsome and ill-tempered wife" (Prov. 21:19). And another proverb says, "A quarrelsome wife is like a constant dripping on a rainy day; restraining her is like restraining the wind or grasping oil with the hand" (Prov. 27:15,16).

From the overall story of Joseph's life, I'm confident that these verses *do not* describe Asenath. She evidently was a very supportive wife and mother. Her friendship and love brought healing to Joseph's emotional life. And the sons she bore filled the vacuum in his life and enabled him to forget the deep loneliness he felt all those years when he was so cruelly separated from those he loved. Interestingly, it was Joseph's first family that initially caused him so much pain. And thirteen years later God used Joseph's own family to heal that pain.

It's also clear that Joseph did not allow himself to be influenced by Asenath's pagan background. For one thing, she was the only woman in his life. She was all that Joseph needed emotionally and physically.

In a pagan society and government where men in high positions often demonstrated their power and prestige by the number of women in their harem, this is indeed significant. Joseph did not even follow in the footsteps of his father, Jacob. He maintained a monogamist relationship all his life, knowing this was God's ideal plan for marriage.

Furthermore, his own relationship with God grew and matured. Could we not conclude that Asenath probably became a believer in the one true God, the God of Abraham, Isaac and Jacob—and the God of her husband Joseph?

God was also honoring Joseph's commitment to purity. His relationship with Asenath was legitimate, meaningful and enduring. It was based not upon lust and selfish desire, but upon true love and commitment. This relationship also produced the family that in turn brought additional healing to Joseph's emotional life. *Don't base your marriage on lust*

Joseph now had two important people in his life—his wife Asenath and his firstborn Manasseh. What a joyous day that must have been for Joseph! Just holding that little boy in his arms must have brought incredible emotional healing. And Joseph wanted everyone to know about his healing. Thus, he named him Manasseh and said, "It is because God has made me forget all my trouble and all my father's household" (Gen. 41:51).

EPHRAIM—"GOD HAS MADE ME FRUITFUL"
Genesis 41:52

Asenath bore Joseph a second son. And again Joseph chose a name that focused on what God was doing in his life. *Ephraim* comes from a root word meaning "to be fruitful."

There are two possible interpretations regarding Joseph's intentions in naming his second son Ephraim. By "fruitful" did he mean that God had given him a wife and two sons? Or was he referring to his position and accomplishments in Egypt?

First and foremost he was probably referring to his family. God had made him "fruitful" in giving him two sons. But God had also made him "fruitful" in giving him position, wealth and success in Egypt. Joseph was in the midst of the "seven years of abundance" when his sons were born. The land "produced plentifully." Joseph had already "stored up huge quantities of grain, like the sand of the sea." There was "so much that he stopped keeping records because it was beyond measure" (Gen. 41:47,49). There's only one way to describe what was happening to Joseph both in his family life and in his political life. God had made him "fruitful" in the land of his "suffering."

With this statement Joseph also let us know he had not forgotten what he suffered in Egypt. But he also let us know he was now rejoicing in what God had both allowed and done in his life. He understood both the trial and now his triumph. And his trial only served to make him stronger and more appreciative of God's present blessings and emotional healing in his life.

SOME PERSONAL REFLECTIONS

Joseph's life story demonstrates clearly that at times God allows suffering in the lives of His children to accomplish His own special purposes. In Joseph's case, God was preparing him for a gigantic task. His personal preparation—as we saw in our last chapter—involved some very difficult experiences that would put him on guard against becoming *prideful*, that would enable him to *persevere* in some very demanding circumstances, and that would prepare him to *perform* well when given a gigantic task.

God's more direct purpose, however, was to use Joseph to save countless numbers of people who would have died because of the forthcoming famine (Gen. 50:20). But beyond that, God's ultimate purpose was to bring into being a great nation, Israel, through whom Jesus Christ would eventually come into the world to provide an opportunity for all people everywhere—then and now—to have eternal life. In that sense, it was a very important step in the fulfillment of God's promise to, and covenant with, Joseph's great-grandfather Abraham (Gen. 12:1-3).

In chapter 12 we will discuss a larger perspective on suffering—more specifically, why God's people suffer. At this point, however, it is important to know and understand that it is dangerous to generalize from Joseph's experience, particularly without qualifying the application. To conclude that *all suffering* has purpose similar to Joseph's suffering is not accurate. The facts are that some suffering is directly related to our own mistakes or, in some instances, are beyond our control because of Satan's influences in the world. But whatever the reason for suffering, what we learn from Joseph's experience is the dynamic means God uses to bring emotional healing in our lives. At this point the application becomes universal. Let's begin where God began with Joseph.

1. If God allows us to endure emotional stress in order to prepare us more adequately for His service, He will eventually bring healing into our lives. In fact, we will be stronger than ever and more fruitful in His service.

Job is a classic illustration of one who suffered. His situation, though much different from Joseph, also had some similarities. Job was a "blameless and upright" man who was enormously blessed by God. One day Satan challenged the Lord regarding Job's righteous behavior. "You have blessed the work of his hands," Satan said, "so that his flocks and herds are spread throughout the land. But stretch out your hand and strike everything he has, and he will surely curse you to your face" (Job 1:1,10,11).

God allowed Satan to test Job severely—to remove everything Job had. Item by item, everything Job had was destroyed. He lost all his oxen and donkeys (Job 1:13-15); he lost his sheep (Job 1:16); he lost his camels (Job 1:17). In each case all the servants tending these animals were killed except the one person who reported each catastrophe. And the final blow came as all of his sons and daughters lost their lives when a house collapsed during a violent wind-storm (Job 1:18,19).

Job's reactions were incredible. He fell on his face and worshiped the Lord. "Naked I came from my mother's womb, and naked I will depart," he prayed. "The Lord gave and the Lord has taken away; may the name of the Lord be praised" (Job 1:20,21).

Job's response was above reproach. "In all this," we read, "Job did not sin by charging God with wrongdoing" (Job 1:22).

Predictably, Satan was not satisfied. He challenged the Lord to strike Job's flesh, "And," Satan said, "he will surely curse you to your face" (Job 2:5).

God approved Satan's plan, but forbade Satan to take Job's life. Satan responded by afflicting Job with "painful sores from the soles of his feet to the top of his head" (Job 2:7). Job's wife, seeing him in such a pitiful condition, told him to "curse God and die" (Job 2:9). But again Job passed the test. He "did not sin" against God (Job 2:10).

Job's ordeal was long and painful. Three of his philo-sophical friends tried to convince him that the Lord was judging him because of sin in his life. Though Job wavered and complained about his condition, he never turned against God. He passed the test victoriously and in the end God restored to His servant everything he had lost and more. We read that "the Lord blessed the latter part of Job's life more than the first" (Job 42:12). In fact, God "gave him twice as much as he had before" (Job 42:10).

In Job's life, like Joseph's, God had a special purpose in allowing him to suffer. With Job, it was an unusual demon-stration to Satan and all of us that those who truly believe in God and trust Him can remain true to Him no matter what our earthly circumstances and even though we do not understand *why* we are suffering. For Joseph, it was to pre-pare him for a great task that had not only earthly but eter-nal implications. And in every instance where God allows the righteous to suffer in order to use them in a special way, He will certainly make them stronger and more effective following the trial. This indeed is why God allows it in the first place.

In Paul's experience, we know that God does not always remove every problem associated with the trial. The great apostle was given a vision of eternal things that was so overwhelming that God allowed a "thorn" in Paul's flesh. We don't know what the thorn was, but we know its purpose was to keep Paul "from becoming conceited" (2 Cor. 12:7).

Three times Paul asked the Lord to remove the thorn. But the Lord's response was that His "grace" was "sufficient" and that His "power" would be "made perfect in weakness" (2 Cor. 12:8,9). Thus God did not remove all of Paul's problem but provided strength to handle his problem and to be a more effective servant of Christ in the process.

Thus we can emphasize again that if God allows us to go through a painful experience in order to prepare us more adequately for His service, He will restore to us all that we need to serve Him and to carry out His purposes in this life.

2. No matter what the cause of our suffering, God can bring about emotional healing by using other people in our lives.

A marital partner—for Joseph it was, first of all, his wife. And how true today. Many men and women have experienced emotional healing because of a loving and sensitive wife or husband. And most men who have achieved anything at all have done so because of faithful wives who have stood behind them, believing in them, and supporting them. But there are also men who either have failed or at least have not measured up to their potential because of wives who were unsupportive. Rather than building up their husbands they have torn them down, competed with them, manipulated them, and punished them in various ways. The end result, of course, is devastating to both.

Children—Joseph's healing was also related to his children. His sons filled a real vacuum in his life and caused him to forget his painful past. And thus our own children can do the same. There is nothing more blessed and encouraging than children who grow up loving God and their parents. On the other hand, there is nothing more devastating to our emotional well-being than children who do the opposite.

Several proverbs speak clearly to this point. We read, "My son, if your heart is wise, then *my heart will be glad;* my inmost being will *rejoice* when your lips speak what is right" (Prov. 23:15,16). And again, "The father of a righteous man has *great joy;* he who has a wise son delights in him" (Prov. 23:24). And finally, the author states this wish and prayer for all children, "May your *father* and *mother* be glad; may she who gave you birth rejoice!" (Prov. 23:25).

On the other hand the Proverbs also tell us that children who do not walk in God's ways bring "grief" to their parents (Prov. 10:1; 15:20). One day a Christian mother approached me with a broken heart. Her daughter, who was in her twenties, had been through a divorce. Both parents tried to help her by setting her up in her own apartment, giving her money to pay her rent and to care for her personal needs. Five years later they discovered she had squandered thousands of dollars they gave her with her immoral friends, engaging in worldly activities.

At that point they stopped supporting her. She left town, found her ex-husband and lived with him until he eventually threw her out. She then returned to her parents, began collecting a welfare check, continued to spend it on wasteful living and at the same time sponged off her parents. She refused to work, she refused to help around the house, and she refused to abide by her parents' standards of right and wrong.

This mother was indeed distressed. "What can we do?" she asked. And of course it pained my own heart as well as hers to tell her that they must not continue to allow her to use them and to manipulate them in this way. The most loving thing they could do would be to stop her from living an irresponsible life, no matter what it took to get the point across.

After that very difficult encounter, my wife and I talked about how wonderful it is to have children who respond with gratitude and love. It is a great blessing and often one that we take for granted.

For Joseph, his own two sons became a healing force in his life. They no doubt reminded him of his early years when he felt secure and loved in the family setting.

The family of God—is yet another perspective. It's God's wonderful plan regarding the church. God has designed that every local body of believers be a healing community of love and acceptance. In that sense the family of God becomes a reparenting experience for people who are hurting deeply from rejection and other difficult experiences. That is another story in itself.[1]

A PERSONAL CHALLENGE

I delivered the following message on Valentine's Day. I could not pass up the opportunity to write a letter to my wife and share it publicly with my "larger family"—the church I serve as pastor. I share it with you to encourage you to honor those who have brought emotional healing to your life; that has been true of my wife. To honor her I share with you this tribute:

My Dear Elaine,

It's very appropriate that I share this letter with you this morning—and publicly. First, it's Valentine's Day and second, it relates to the message. Third, so many times as a pastor's wife, you function behind the scenes and few people really know how faithful you are to me, and always have been. And I want everyone to know that without you—your *constant* support, your *encouragement*, your *devotedness* to me and to our children, I could not pastor and lead this church.

In fact, it's been that way for over twenty-five years. I'm thankful particularly for those tough nine years when I was grinding out my doctorate at New York University—being away from you and the children during the summer months. I didn't realize until it was all over how difficult those years were for you. But you hung in there—uncomplaining. Thank you!

I think of our children. They're not perfect but I'm proud of them. And you are the reason. Without your commitment to them all these years, particularly picking up the slack when I've been overwhelmed with other people's problems, and often out of town or working late in the office, they would surely have become disillusioned with me—and Christianity. You've always defended me to them, interpreted my schedule, and reassured them of my love when I was absent or emotionally unable to be everything I wanted to be.

And thanks too for lovingly and boldly confronting me when I've failed to do the things I should have done. But thanks for always doing it face to face, never behind my back and never in front of the children.

I can identify with Joseph. You've often helped me *forget* my problems and you've been the primary secret to any *fruitfulness* in my life. I owe a great debt to you. Thank you!

With love and appreciation,
Gene

Note
1. Consult the author's books entitled *Building Up One Another, Loving One Another, Encouraging One Another, Praying for One Another*—all published by Victor Books, Wheaton, Illinois.

9

Joseph
Faces the Ultimate Test

GENESIS 42:1-28

- Have you ever felt wronged by someone who will not admit that wrong? What is your attitude towards that person?

- What should a Christian's attitudes and actions be towards that person in a situation such as this?

One of the greatest struggles in life is to forgive someone who has wronged us, even though that person has not acknowledged the wrong nor sought forgiveness. And the Bible nowhere indicates that our willingness to forgive should be predicated on the fact that someone has asked forgiveness. Jesus of course set the example nobly when He hung on a rugged cross and cried out, regarding those who had so cruelly nailed Him there, "Father, forgive them, for they know not what they do."

However, one of the greatest temptations to vindicate

ourselves or to retaliate comes when we meet face to face the one who has offended us. At that moment, whether or not we have *truly* forgiven is put to the test. When we are separated from that person it is easier to *forget* the pain and hurt we have experienced and rise above the human tendency to bear a grudge. But when we interface with that person, all the old memories are revived and naturally tend to come to the surface.

Joseph faced that very problem. His brothers had treated him cruelly. Though Joseph was certainly not without fault (we never are), he did not deserve such evil and cruel treatment. But we've seen Joseph's true character and love for his brothers. He held no grudges, nor did he harbor a desire to get even. God had brought healing to his heart and mind, enabling him to "forget" all of his trials in Egypt as well as what happened in Canaan.

But the next major event in Joseph's life relative to his painful experience brought him face to face with his brothers, and with that experience came another test of his character. And what makes Joseph such an outstanding example is that he had every opportunity to retaliate. They had no choice. He was in control and they were at his mercy. He had numerous options. He could have imprisoned them and let them know how it feels to be incarcerated in a strange land with no one to represent your case. He could have sent them back to Canaan without food, leading to a slow but certain death. Or he had the authority to accuse them of spying and to have them executed. How Joseph faced this traumatic confrontation speaks loud and clear to every Christian who wants to follow in the footsteps of Jesus Christ.

JOSEPH'S ENCOUNTER WITH HIS BROTHERS
Genesis 42:1-8

The famine Joseph predicted came not only to Egypt but it spread throughout the then known world (Gen. 41:57).

Consequently, Joseph's homeland, Canaan, was severely affected. And the word also began to spread—thanks to Joseph's storehouse operation—that there was "grain in Egypt" (Gen. 42:2). Consequently, Jacob sent his sons to Egypt to buy food.

Ironically, after twenty years of separation, God used the famine to bring the sons of Jacob face to face with their brother Joseph. Arriving in Egypt to see if they could buy grain, they were ushered into his presence. Imagine for a moment what must have gone through Joseph's mind or heart when he looked up and saw ten men bowing low before him. Their garb was readily recognizable. Their tan, weather-beaten faces were those of shepherds and their beards set them off from the clean-shaven Egyptian men. Instantly, Joseph knew who they were—his brothers (Gen. 42:7)!

Joseph Unrecognized

Though Joseph recognized them, he also sensed they did not know who he was. After all, he was only seventeen when they last saw him—and now he was nearly forty. Since most of his brothers were all relatively mature in age when they sold him into Egypt, their physical changes were minor compared with Joseph's. Furthermore, Joseph was now clean-shaven. His hairstyle reflected the Egyptian culture and he stood before them in royal garb. It is understandable they did not recognize him. Furthermore, in their own minds he was dead!

Very quickly, Joseph must have surveyed them. There stood Reuben, the oldest. And there was Simeon, Levi, Judah, Issachar and Zebulun—all sons of Leah. No doubt standing together were Dan and Napthali—sons of Bilhah, along with Dan and Asher, sons of Zilpah. But *where* was his youngest brother Benjamin, who was also the son of his own mother, Rachel?

Joseph's Questions

What were Joseph's thoughts and emotions at that moment? We can only speculate. They certainly would have been mixed. On the one hand he probably had an intense desire to reveal his identity. On the other hand that approach would not answer the questions that were flooding his mind. What were their attitudes *now*? Had they changed? Were their hearts soft and tender towards God? What was their relationship with their father? Was Jacob even alive? And, more important to Joseph than anything, he wanted to know about his younger brother Benjamin. Where was he? Was he still alive? Had they treated Benjamin like they had treated him? Had they transferred their jealousy and anger to Benjamin once Joseph disappeared off the scene? Was it possible that they had actually taken his life as they had once planned to do to Joseph?

Joseph's Flashback

In a moment like this the mind does strange things! Details of events that happened years before are often condensed into an instantaneous flashback. Seeing his brothers bowing down before him, faces to the ground, suddenly took him back over twenty years to where his troubles actually began. He remembered his own dreams that had created such intense jealousy and hatred. The first dream involved sheaves of grain. Joseph was in the field binding those sheaves and suddenly his sheaf "rose and stood upright" and his brothers' sheaves gathered around him and "bowed down to it" (Gen. 37:7). In the second dream, "the son and moon and eleven stars" bowed down to Joseph (Gen. 41:9). In his naiveté, Joseph had shared these dreams with his brothers and his father. Though unaware of the prophetic and supernatural significance of these dreams, it became very clear to Jacob and his sons that Joseph—in his mind—was occupying some kind of position over them (Gen. 37:10,11).

And now, twenty-two years later, it was happening! His brothers *were* bowing down before him. He *was* in a position of honor over them. And for Joseph, another piece—a big piece—of the puzzle fit. In fact, what happened that day became a key in unlocking Joseph's understanding regarding *why* God had allowed him to be sold into Egypt. Remembering the dreams and seeing God's purpose in it all must have dissipated any anger that would naturally emerge in that moment. Any temptation to retaliate would be quickly disregarded for more noble actions.

JOSEPH'S LEGITIMATE CONCERNS
Genesis 42:7-13

Joseph did have legitimate concerns! After all, his brothers had not acted righteously on *numerous* occasions (Gen. 37:2). Not only had they mistreated him, but they had little regard for the negative impact their actions would have on their aging father. And what about Benjamin? It would be natural for Jacob to focus his attention and affection on Joseph's little brother when he assumed that his favorite son was killed by a wild animal.

Joseph needed some answers to his questions. Consequently he acted as if he didn't know them and "spoke harshly to them," not to retaliate but to try to discover what was going on in their hearts and minds. "Where do you come from?" he asked, pretending "to be a stranger" (Gen. 42:7).

Their response of course was predictable. They told Joseph they were from Canaan and had come "to buy food" (Gen. 42:7). Forcing himself, Joseph shouted, "You are spies! You have come to see where our land is unprotected" (Gen. 42:9). And with this accusation Joseph was implying they could be imprisoned and executed.

Understandably, Joseph's brothers were shocked! Defending themselves they repeated why they were there. But Joseph asked more pointed questions that are not recorded in this chapter. At this juncture he must have asked the questions that the brothers later reported to their father. "The man [referring to Joseph] questioned us closely about ourselves and our family. 'Is you father still living?' he asked us. 'Do you have another brother?' " (Gen. 43:7).

Their answer to these questions must have set Joseph's heart pounding with relief and ecstasy. "Your servants were twelve brothers, the sons of one man, who *lives* in the land of Canaan. The youngest is *now* with our father, and one is *no more*" (Gen. 42:13).

Jacob was alive! And so was Benjamin! And in their thinking he, Joseph, was dead. But what about their own attitudes? Had they changed? How were they treating Benjamin?

JOSEPH'S PLAN EVOLVES
Genesis 42:14-28

Joseph needed more information before he could let them know who he really was. Consequently, he continued to force himself to challenge their responses. "You are spies!" Joseph repeated. But he told them he would test them to see if they were telling the truth. "You will not leave this place unless your youngest brother comes here" (Gen. 42:15).

A Painful Nerve

Their hearts must have sunk. Joseph had touched a sore spot. Jacob had not sent Benjamin in the first place "because he was afraid that harm might come to him" (Gen. 42:4). And here we learn something of what had happened when their father had received the report of Joseph's death. Jacob's affection and love *had* focused on Benjamin. He became the favorite son. And since that time, Jacob probably never trusted his welfare to his other sons. Perhaps in his heart he had often wondered what *really* had happened to Joseph. After all, their jealousy and hatred had been obvious. Though Jacob had ignored it at the time, in retrospect there is no way he would not have remembered it.

Furthermore, guilt has a way of coming to the surface. For over twenty years Jacob's sons had tried to hide their guilt—a very difficult thing for ten men to do in an extended family. Living together with their wives and children during this period of time, it would have been a miracle if one or several of these men had not let something slip at some moment—particularly while lingering too long at their wine.

Whatever had happened in the twenty-year interval, that moment in Joseph's court in Egypt brought to the surface memories these men had tried to forget. And Joseph's next ultimatum threatened them even more. "Send one of your number to get your brother; the rest of you will be kept in prison, so that your words may be tested to see if you are telling the truth. If you are not, then as surely as Pharaoh lives, you are spies!" (Gen. 42:16).

Time to Reflect

At this juncture, Joseph needed time to think! What should he do next? Consequently, he "put them all in custody for three days" (Gen. 42:17). During that time he must have evaluated his ultimatum. It was too severe! Perhaps he thought of his aged father. Seeing only one son return while the others were imprisoned in Egypt may have been more than his father's old heart could handle. And furthermore, Jacob may not have believed the one returned son.

During that three-day period, Joseph no doubt reflected on the answers his brothers had given during the interrogation. There was one obvious omission. They had evidently said nothing about God. What were their attitudes toward Him? Had they continued all these years to violate His commandments and will? Had they softened their hearts and developed spiritually? Were their consciences still seared and hardened?

A Revised Plan

Joseph changed his plan. In reporting that change, he decided to test their attitude towards God. He let them know that he—a high-ranking Egyptian official—believed and served the same God they worshiped. "Do this and you will live, for *I* fear God," he said. "If you are honest men, let one of your brothers stay here in prison, while the rest of you go and take grain back for your starving households. But you *must* bring your youngest brother to me, so that your words may be verified and that you may *not die*" (Gen. 42:18-20). And with this final statement he indicated that their own lives may be at stake if they did not cooperate. Furthermore, Joseph was correlating in their thinking that belief in God and His laws should create a healthy fear of purposely violating His will.

Awakened Consciences

Joseph's strategy worked. God began to awaken their seared consciences through Joseph's words. They began to see a connection between what was happening to them in Egypt and what they had done to Joseph years before. "Surely we are being punished because of our brother," they said to one another. "We saw how distressed he was when he pleaded with us for his life, but we would not listen; that's why this distress has come upon us" (Gen. 42:21).

Reuben, the oldest, became even more specific. "Didn't I tell you not to sin against the boy? But you wouldn't listen! Now we must give an accounting for his blood" (Gen. 42:22).

Though they did not realize it, Joseph understood every word they were saying. For the first time in his encounter with his brothers he began to get answers to the most important questions he was concerned about. Were his brothers aware of their sin? More specifically, were they sorry for what they had done? Were they reflecting a different attitude towards Benjamin and their father or had they continued in their selfish, jealous behavior? He now knew that his father lived and that Benjamin was still at home and evidently well.

At that moment he began to see their hearts soften. He could not bear any longer to stand and watch their expressions and listen to their conversations. His own heart was responding with deep emotion. He left their presence and "began to weep," no doubt reflecting—not sadness—but joy (Gen. 42:24).

But Joseph quickly regained control of himself and determined that it was not yet time to reveal his identity. Though he was confident their hearts were beginning to change, he was not yet sure of their motives. It is one thing to admit guilt when caught in your own web. It's another thing to admit guilt because you are truly sorry for what you've done. For Joseph's brothers it seemed to be more the former than the latter.

Joseph probably had to force himself to stick to his plan. But he did! He retained Simeon and sent the other nine back to Canaan with their bags filled with grain. Unknown to them he had given instructions to "put each man's silver back in his sack." That night when they stopped to rest, one of them discovered the money. The results were dramatic, and traumatic for Joseph's brothers. "Their hearts sank and they turned to each other trembling and said, 'What is this that God has done to us?' " (Gen. 42:28).

They were now sure and admitted that *God* was involved in this whole episode. They were sincerely frightened. How could they explain all of this to their father? Were they being forced to reveal all they had done to their brother Joseph? Would their father even allow them to take Benjamin to Egypt, especially if he suspected what they had *really* done to Joseph? Furthermore, what would happen if they did return to Egypt? How could they explain the returned money to the Egyptian ruler? And at this point they didn't even know that the money each had paid was in *every* sack of grain! (Gen. 42:35).

Joseph's brothers found themselves in a serious dilemma, as most people eventually do when they sin and try to cover it up. It may even take years for the results of that sin to come to full fruition, but it will happen. And the longer we live in that situation with that sin unconfessed and unrepented, the more complex and complicated the results. What we see happening to Joseph's brothers certainly and dramatically illustrates that reality.

SOME PERSONAL REFLECTIONS

There is no evidence in this story that Joseph was attempting to vindicate himself or retaliate for what his brothers had done to him. Rather, he was deeply concerned about his father and particularly about his younger brother Benjamin. He had long since forgiven his brothers for what they had done to him, no matter what their ongoing spiritual state. But in this instance he still faced some hard realities regarding how their present attitudes and behavior may still be affecting others. Consequently, he could not be totally open with them, though his heart cried out to do so.

Furthermore, it's obvious Joseph was deeply concerned about his brothers' spiritual welfare. More important than their attitudes towards him were their attitudes towards God and His laws of righteousness. Their awakened consciences caused Joseph to weep. True, there must have been added healing in his own heart to hear them admit their wrongdoing towards him, but Joseph's tears seemed more related to what was happening in their own hearts. His example speaks directly to us today.

1. When someone wrongs us, we are to forgive unconditionally even though that person may not admit it was wrong or ask forgiveness. It is clear from Scripture that we

are to forgive others as Christ forgave us (Col. 3:13). And Christ forgave us before we ever asked Him to. We simply received the benefits of that forgiveness when we accepted His gift of eternal life.

NOTE: If we have contributed to any wrongdoing we should lead out and confess our own wrongdoing and seek forgiveness.

2. Forgiveness of those who have wronged us but who do not admit it does not mean that a relationship will be completely restored. However, God can use our own non-vindictive attitudes and behavior to eventually bring conviction to that person regarding his own wrongdoing. In this way we can "overcome evil with good" (Rom. 12:21).

3. One method God uses to help people see their wrongdoing and to come to the place they can admit it is to allow them to experience the same pain they have caused someone else. However, this must happen according to God's timing, not ours!

4. When we have been wronged by someone who has not admitted it or sought forgiveness, we should have two primary concerns that guide our attitudes and behavior: (1) their own relationship with God, and (2) how their ongoing behavior is affecting others.

NOTE: At this point we must be very careful to evaluate our own motives. We can very quickly rationalize our own behavior, and what appears to be concern for their own spirituality and concern for others can actually be a subtle way to retaliate!

A true test of our motives in situations such as this is the degree to which we talk to God about the person rather than how much we talk to others. The place to start is with prayer, not asking God to vindicate us (though this is not in itself wrong), but rather to ask God to help that person to regain proper perspective spiritually. If we do, perhaps God will open the door of opportunity to be a part of that person's restoration. And if that door opens—as it did with

Joseph—we'll soon find out how much we have actually forgiven that person. Furthermore, if *God* has opened the door, our part in the process will be natural, not forced!

A PERSONAL CHALLENGE

If you identify with any of these lessons, take steps necessary to be in the will of God.

1. Unconditionally forgive those who have trespassed against you.

NOTE: For the most part, this must be an act of the will, not the emotions.

2. If you have forgiven a person under these circumstances, don't expect instant restoration. It may take years.

3. Allow God to work out the restoration in His own time. Don't force the process.

4. Begin today to pray regularly: (1) for that person's spiritual restoration; (2) that God would protect others from that person's wrongdoing.

NOTE: Begin your prayers by admitting your own weaknesses and failures.

ANOTHER LESSON FROM CORRIE

I wish I could say that after a long and fruitful life, traveling the world, I had learned to forgive all my enemies. I wish I could say that merciful and charitable thoughts just naturally flowed from me and on to others. But they don't. If there is one thing I've learned since I've passed my eightieth birthday, it's that I can't store up good feelings and behavior—but only draw them fresh from God each day.

Maybe I'm glad it's that way, for every time I go to Him, He teaches me something else. I recall the time—and I was almost seventy—when some Christian friends whom I loved and trusted did something which hurt me. You would have thought that, having been able to forgive the guards in Ravensbruck, forgiving Christian friends would be child's play. It wasn't. For weeks I seethed inside. But at last I asked God again to work His miracle in me. And again it happened: first the cold-blooded decision, then the flood of joy and peace. I had forgiven my friends; I was restored to my Father.

Then, why was I suddenly awake in the middle of the night, rehashing the whole affair again? My friends! I thought. People I loved. If it had been strangers, I wouldn't have minded so.

I sat up and switched on the light. "Father, I thought it was all forgiven. Please help me do it."

But the next night I woke up again. They'd talked so sweetly too! Never a hint of what they were planning. "Father!" I cried in alarm. "Help me!"

Then it was that another secret of forgiveness became evident. It is not enough to simply say, "I forgive you." I must also begin to live it out. And in my case, that meant acting as though their sins, like mine, were buried in the depths of the deepest sea. If God could remember them no more—and He had said, "(Your) sins and iniquities will I remember no more" (Heb. 10:17)—then neither should I. And the reason the thoughts kept coming back to me was that I kept turning their sin over in my mind.

And so I discovered another of God's principles: We can trust God not only for our emotions but also for our thoughts. As I asked Him to renew my mind He also took away my thoughts.

He still had more to teach me, however, even from this single episode. Many years later, after I had passed my eightieth birthday, an American friend came to visit me in Holland. As we sat in my little apartment in Baarn he asked me about those people from long ago who had taken advantage of me.

"It is nothing," I said a little smugly. "It is all forgiven."

"By you, yes," he said. "But what about them? Have they accepted your forgiveness?"

"They say there is nothing to forgive! They deny it ever happened. No matter what they say, though, I can prove they were wrong." I went eagerly to my desk. "See, I have it in black and white! I saved all their letters and I can show you where . . ."

"Corrie!" My friend slipped his arm through mine and gently closed the drawer. "Aren't you the one whose sins are at the bottom of the sea? Yet are the sins of your friends etched in black and white?"

For an astonishing moment I could not find my voice. "Lord Jesus," I whispered at last, "who takes all my sins away, forgive me for preserving all these years the evidence against others! Give me grace to burn all the blacks and whites as a sweet-smelling sacrifice to Your glory."

I did not go to sleep that night until I had gone through my desk and pulled out those letters—curling now with age—and fed them all into my little coal-burning grate. As the flames leaped and glowed, so did my heart. "Forgive us our trespasses," Jesus taught us to pray, "as we forgive those who trespass against us." In the ashes of those letters I was seeing yet another facet of His mercy. What more He would teach me about forgiveness in the days ahead I didn't know, but tonight's was good news enough.

Forgiveness is the key which unlocks the door of resentment and the handcuffs of hatred. It breaks the chains of bitterness and the shackles of selfishness. The forgiveness of Jesus not only takes away our sins, it makes them as if they had never been.[1]

Note
1. Corrie Ten Boom, *Tramp for the Lord*, pp. 181-183.

10

Joseph's
Questions Answered

GENESIS 42:37-44:34

- What mistakes do people make in human relationships that destroy trust?

- How can trust be reestablished?

- What experiences have you had in attempting to reestablish trust?

To this point in Joseph's encounter with his brothers, he has been able to discover answers to several important questions. Yes, his father Jacob was still alive! Yes, his brother Benjamin was still living at home. At least they had not killed him or sold him as a slave. And yes, his brothers knew in their hearts that they had sinned against God when they sinned against their brother Joseph. Down deep they were still haunted by that stern reality (Gen. 42:21)!

But there were still several unanswered questions in

Joseph's mind. The answers to those questions were more important to Joseph than any other answers. They involved attitudes and actions towards Benjamin, towards their father Jacob and most important, towards God Himself. Were his brothers still controlled by jealousy? Were they still insensitive towards their father's feelings? And were their consciences still hardened toward God and His righteous laws? Before Joseph felt free to reveal who he really was, he *had* to have answers to these questions!

In this chapter we'll see he got answers to all these questions which freed Joseph up to reveal his identity. But more important, he was free in his spirit to do something for them he had wanted to do from the very first time he saw them after a long twenty-two-year interval.

But that's getting ahead of the story. Let's look at the dramatic process that finally surfaced the answers to Joseph's questions.

REUBEN'S ATTEMPT TO REESTABLISH TRUST
Genesis 42:37,38

When Joseph's brothers returned to Canaan they reported to their father everything that had transpired in Egypt (Gen. 42:29-35), including the fact that if they wanted any more grain, they would have to return with their youngest brother Benjamin. And while "they were emptying their sacks" of grain they discovered that the silver they used to pay for the grain was in *every* sack. They were overwhelmed with fear!

Jacob's response to all of this was predictable. "You have deprived me of my children," he said. "Joseph is no more and Simeon is no more, and now you want to take Benjamin. Everything is against me!" (Gen. 42:36). Chuck Swindoll identifies this section as "the groanings of a sad dad"!

At this juncture, Reuben, Jacob's oldest, wasted no time in conveying Joseph's message to his father. He attempted to convince Jacob to allow Benjamin to return to Egypt. His offer was startling but irrational. "You may put both of my sons to death if I do not bring him back to you. Entrust him to my care," Reuben pleaded, "and I will bring him back" (Gen. 42:37).

Jacob of course would never have taken the life of his two grandsons, no matter what happened. But it shows the frustration Reuben felt at that moment. It also shows the extent to which he had felt untrusted by his father all those years. How many times he must have heard Jacob repeat the words, "I'll never entrust one of my sons to you again! You, Reuben, are the oldest! You are responsible because of your very position in the family. Yet you allowed my son Joseph to be attacked and killed by a wild animal! No, Reuben, never again!" Furthermore, Jacob had probably reminded Reuben many times—if not overtly, covertly—that he had betrayed his trust by defiling his father's bed. That, Jacob never forgot—even to his dying day (Gen. 49:4)!

This lack of trust must have weighed heavily on Reuben. Regarding Joseph's plight he would have felt it was unfair. After all, he was the one who had "tried to rescue" Joseph "from their hands." His plan was to remove his brother from the cistern and "take him back to his father" (Gen. 37:21,22). But his lips had been sealed all these years! He had become part of a deceptive plot and there was no way to communicate to his father his initial intentions without exposing his brothers—and himself! Consequently, being the oldest he had to bear final responsibility for Joseph's welfare in spite of his efforts to save him.

His offer to allow Jacob to take the lives of his own two sons if he did not prove trustworthy was a desperate effort to regain his father's trust and his position in the family. But once again it didn't work! Once again he felt that deep rejection when Jacob wouldn't budge. "My son will *not* go down there with you," Jacob responded. "His brother is dead and he is the only one left. If harm comes to him on the journey you are taking, you will bring my gray head down to the grave in sorrow" (Gen. 42:38).

From this point in the biblical narrative Reuben becomes just one of the brothers, and his name does not appear specifically until later when his father—in his final days—reminds Reuben that he would *never* regain his position of honor in the family, particularly because of his incestuous actions. It is a pathetic reminder that in some situations we can make mistakes that in some respects take us beyond the point of no return in certain human relationships. There seems to be no way to rebuild trust, no matter what our efforts. Thank God, those are rare circumstances. But it is a solemn warning to all of us!

JUDAH STEPS FORWARD AND TAKES LEADERSHIP
Genesis 43:1-14

For a brief period of time there seems to have been no discussion between Jacob and his sons regarding Joseph's ultimatum to bring Benjamin to Egypt. But the circumstances surrounding the famine did not allow the matter to lie dormant. Jacob himself brought up the matter when their supply of grain was depleted. "Go back and buy us a little more food," he said (Gen. 43:2).

This time Judah, the second oldest, emerged as the spokesman. He reviewed again for his father what the Egyptian ruler had said—that they would not even get an audience with him if they did not return with Benjamin. "If you will not send him, we will not go down," Judah stated (Gen. 43:5).

Judah also offered to be responsible for Benjamin. Communicating more rationally than Reuben, he told his father that he would personally "bear the blame" before Jacob the rest of his life if he did not bring Benjamin back safely (Gen. 43:9). Reluctantly, and after what appears to have been a rather intense argument, Jacob finally consented. He saw he had no choice if they were to survive the famine. He instructed his sons to take some gifts to the Egyptian ruler and to take enough money to pay back what was returned in their sacks of grain as well as enough to pay for a new supply. Though deeply distressed over the fact he had to make this decision, Jacob hoped against hope that perhaps God would bring them all back safely (Gen. 43:11-14).

JOSEPH MEETS BENJAMIN FACE TO FACE
Genesis 43:15-34

When Jacob's sons arrived in Egypt, to their surprise they were ushered into Joseph's private mansion. Gripped with fear they thought they were going to be charged with stealing the silver they had found in their sacks and then taken captive as slaves. They wasted no time seeking out Joseph's steward—the man who had handled the transaction initially—to explain what happened. They showed him the money they brought back. Imagine their surprise and relief when the steward told them not to worry. He remembered having received their silver. And imagine too what must have gone through their minds when he said, "Your God and the God of your father has given you treasure in your sacks" (Gen. 43:23).

Here was a polytheistic Egyptian talking about *their* God and the God of *their father*. The facts are that the name of God had probably been mentioned more frequently by the Egyptians than He had been in Jacob's own family gatherings over the past twenty years. After all, when you're in violation of God's commands and will—as Joseph's brothers were—you usually don't want to talk about spiritual things.

When Joseph arrived home they already had the gifts laid out to present to him. Though grateful I'm sure, Joseph quickly zeroed in on his greatest concern, "How is your aged father you told me about? Is he still living?" (Gen. 43:27). Even though Joseph had changed his plan to keep only one of the brothers in Egypt, he no doubt spent some sleepless nights wondering if his father's old heart could handle the strain of having to send Benjamin to Egypt. Joseph's own heart must have been relieved when they responded that their father was "still alive and well" (Gen. 43:28).

This was the moment Joseph had been waiting for. Hardly able to contain his emotions he once more surveyed the scene before him. His eyes quietly fell on the youngest—a twenty-three-year-old. There was no way he could have recognized Benjamin except by his features. The last time Joseph had seen Benjamin, he was only a toddling one-year-old. "Is this your youngest brother, the one you told me about?" Joseph asked, trying to control his emotions. Wanting to throw his arms around Benjamin, Joseph restrained himself and somehow uttered the words—"God be gracious to you, my son" (Gen. 43:29).

However, meeting Benjamin after those many years of separation was too much for Joseph. He could not maintain his emotional control. He was "deeply moved at the sight of his brother" (Gen. 43:30). But he also maintained sufficient rational control to know that this was not yet the time to reveal his identity. He quickly turned, "hurried out" and "went into his private room and wept there" (Gen. 43:30).

Joseph finally regained control of himself. He returned and ordered food served. The brothers were seated before him, and to their astonishment, they were seated one by one in chronological order, "from the firstborn to the youngest." And when the food was served from Joseph's own table their astonishment must have been almost humorous when "Benjamin's portion was *five times* as much as anyone else's" (Gen. 43:33,34).

It was not unusual in certain countries to serve a person who occupied a place of honor larger portions at a special banquet. It was a privilege reserved for princes and rulers. For example, among the Spartans, they *doubled* the portions, and the Cretans served *four times* the usual amount.[1] Joseph outdid himself to make a point. He served Benjamin *five times* more than any of his other brothers.

If the sons of Jacob had any inkling who Joseph was they would have put two and two together by now. How had Joseph known their ages? And the special attention he gave Benjamin was certainly obvious. He was treating him like a prince. But they showed no signs of knowing they were seated in front of their brother Joseph.

It is now clear that Joseph was deeply concerned about his brothers' jealous attitudes and behavior, that had erupted twenty years ago, resulting in such intense hatred that they wanted to take his life. Had they changed? Or had they simply transferred that hatred to Benjamin? Imagine how intently Joseph must have studied their faces and their overall body language while Benjamin was being treated so royally. He must also have strained his ears to pick up the bits and pieces of communication that must have gone on among his brothers when Benjamin was served five times more than they. What he saw and heard no doubt pleased him.

But how could he be sure? And before he felt free to reveal his identity and to unveil his ultimate plan, he *had* to be sure. There was one more step he felt he had to take. It would be the ultimate test of their true hearts and attitudes towards their father and their younger brother.

BENJAMIN ACCUSED OF STEALING
Genesis 44:1-14

When Jacob's sons were ready to leave for Canaan, Joseph instructed his steward to give them as much food as they could carry, to once again return their money, *and* to put his own personal silver cup in Benjamin's sack. Once they were on the way he sent his steward after them to accuse them of stealing.

Predictably, they were dumbfounded. They were so sure of their innocence they offered the life of the one who had done such a thing. They quickly opened their sacks to prove they were not guilty. But to their astonishment, there was Joseph's silver cup in Benjamin's sack! They were so frustrated and distraught that they literally "tore their clothes" (Gen. 44:13).

Joseph's brothers were facing their greatest test. Joseph had no doubt instructed the steward to tell them *before* he conducted his investigation that whoever had the cup would become a slave and the rest were free to go. If they had been jealous of Benjamin when he was treated so royally at the banquet they *may* have been able to mask their feelings. After all, they had done a pretty good job of covering their guilt for over twenty years. But they would not hide their true feelings now! Twenty-two years ago, there was no question what they would have done. And Judah would have taken the lead in suggesting that Benjamin bear the blame and become a slave. Their father's grief over it all would not have been a consideration. But their reactions this time were different! *Together* they returned to Egypt.

Imagine Joseph's relief and joy when he saw their little parade of donkeys enter the palace gates. With heads bowed low, their garments torn, and their long-flowing hair and full beards matted because of the mixture of dust and tears that flowed from their eyes, they were a pathetic sight. But to Joseph they now represented men who were more concerned about their aged father and their younger brother than they were concerned about themselves. They had passed the test.

But there was one who had passed the test even more nobly than the others. His name was Judah!

JUDAH'S REPENTANT CONFESSION
Genesis 44:15-34

When the brothers were ushered into Joseph's house, Judah stepped forward. He made no excuse, gave no rationalizations, and made no attempts to cover up their sinful actions that spanned the twenty-year period. "What can we say?" he said. "How can we prove our innocence?" And he then uttered his most repentant statement to date—"*God has uncovered your servants' guilt.*"

With this confession, Judah acknowledged their sin against Joseph. Though Judah did not mention Joseph's name it was easy to read between the lines. But more important to Joseph was Judah's statement, "*We* are now my lord's slaves—*we* ourselves and the one who was found to have the cup" (Gen. 44:16). Judah made it clear they would not forsake Benjamin. If he were enslaved they would *all* be enslaved. Though *innocent* of the charge of stealing, Judah was acknowledging that they were *guilty* of a much greater sin. And *God* had uncovered that sin.

The fact that Judah acknowledged that God Himself had uncovered their sin is also very significant. They did not see it as *Joseph's* strategy or pressure tactics. Behind it all they recognized God's sovereign intervention. This of course also points to the fact that Joseph was an instrument for righteousness in the hand of God. And it also verifies the wisdom in Joseph's decision to remain anonymous. It served as a divine means in lowering their human defenses.

As Joseph listened to Judah's confession he must have yearned to enfold Judah in his arms and weep with joy. Yet he restrained himself. He had one more question in his mind that was yet unanswered. *How did Judah—and his older brothers—actually feel about Jacob at this moment? What concern did they have for their aged father?* Consequently, Joseph responded to Judah's confession by telling him that "only the man who was found to have the cup" would become his slave. "The rest of you," he continued, can "go back to your father in peace" (Gen. 44:17).

Judah's response was immediate and heartwarming! He focused his thoughts on their father. He reviewed Jacob's response when they had returned from Egypt to Canaan the first time. "If the boy is not with us when I go back to your servant my father," Judah continued, "and if my father, whose life is closely bound up with the boy's life, sees that the boy isn't there, he will die. Your servants will bring the gray head of our father down to the grave in sorrow" (Gen. 44:30,31).

Judah then took the final step in his confession. It was a true sign of personal repentance. He pleaded with Joseph to set Benjamin and his other brothers free and he would personally take his little brother's place as a slave. "How can I go back to my father if the boy is not with me?" he asked. He then answered his own question, "No! Do not let me see the misery that would come upon my father" (Gen. 44:34).

Joseph could stand it no longer. He now had the answer to his final question—and more! Here stood the man who had convinced his brothers to sell him as a slave now offering to be a slave in Benjamin's place. Here stood the man who twenty years ago could have cared less about the impact Joseph's death would have on his father. But now he was so concerned about his father that he was willing to take Benjamin's place as a slave. *This was true repentance!*

JOSEPH REVEALS HIS IDENTITY
Genesis 45:1-3

Hearing Judah's final statement, Joseph could contain himself no longer. He had everyone ushered from the room except his brothers. There he revealed himself, weeping so loudly he could be heard even beyond the confines of his mansion. His brothers were so shocked and terrified they could not utter a word and initially could not accept it as a reality. But what happened that day in that room is in itself another story—to be continued in the next chapter. For now, let's look carefully at what these events just presented say to us today.

SOME PERSONAL REFLECTIONS

There are several significant lessons that flow out of these events which can impact our lives in a special way.

1. We must carefully guard human relationships. These relationships are fragile, particulary in a family setting. Reuben learned the hard way. Though he tried hard he could not right the wrong with his father.

True, Jacob too was at fault. But what we see is a reality. We cannot predict how other people will respond to our mistakes and even our efforts at reconciliation. And often when people don't respond as we would like, we can turn even more bitter, which only increases our frustration and sense of alienation.

There are at least three additional lessons that relate to this reality.

• We must think of the consequences *before* we act. If we do, we'll not do certain things.

• If we have acted, we must *accept* the consequences without allowing those consequences to drive us to do things which will only create more frustration and alienation.

• We must confess our total sin—something Reuben did not do. No matter what the consequences he would have fared better in the long run if he had confessed all of his sins to his father.

2. Total repentance and taking responsibility for mistakes always brings results, no matter what the mistakes. Judah illustrates this point dramatically. He had been a primary leader in convincing his brothers to sell Joseph as a slave. And he took the primary leadership in righting the wrong. He did not blame his father, though certainly Jacob was guilty of showing favoritism. He did not blame his brothers, though they certainly contributed their share of wrongness. He did not blame Joseph, though he certainly could have pointed to his young brother's pride. And most important he didn't blame God. He made no excuses!

God honors a straightforward confession without self-justification and personal rationalizations. We will always be able to find points with which we can defend ourselves.

However, if we have been wrong, we have been wrong. We should not concentrate at that moment on what we've done right, but on our sins and mistakes. God always honors that approach.

3. God is still sovereign in the affairs of men. If we'll let Him, in some marvelous way He can even take our mistakes and our sins and bring good out of evil. This we'll see in a greater way in our next chapter.

A PERSONAL CHALLENGE

There are two approaches we need to take in facing life's challenges. One is *preventative* and the other is *corrective*.

1. To what extent am I helping *prevent* mistakes in my own life and in the lives of others?

NOTE: This is particularly important for parents. Try as we might, we cannot prevent certain mistakes in the lives of our children. They often have to learn the hard way. However, one of the best methods to prevent mistakes in their lives is by our own example. We *cannot force conformity*, but we *can model consistency*. This is a strong force in communicating proper Christian values.

2. To what extent am I *correcting* mistakes in my life? Fortunately most of our mistakes are not as serious as the ones made by Joseph's brothers. In most situations we can go a long way in correcting the results of our mistakes and go on to greater things, if we'll learn from those experiences.

Remember: God does not turn His back on a broken and contrite heart. And neither do most people. Those who do are eventually headed for the same painful experiences in their own relationships with others.

Note
1. Alfred Edersheim, *Old Testament Bible History* (Grand Rapids: Wm. B. Eerdmans Publishing Company, 1977), p. 168.

11

Joseph
Reveals His Heart

GENESIS 45:1-24

- In what way does weeping reveal a person's heart?

- How does culture affect this God-created capacity?

- When was the last time you wept because of another person's spiritual and emotional pain?

When Judah reached the final step in his repentant confession, actually pleading that he be allowed to take Benjamin's place as a slave, Joseph "could no longer control himself" (Gen. 45:1). The powerful urge to reveal his identity, which almost gained control on several previous occasions, now overwhelmed him. Though he was now emotionally out of control, he knew this was the time to take that step. His questions were all answered. His brothers *were* concerned about Benjamin! What jealousy they may have felt was at least under control. Though it would be natural for them to be tempted in this direction, they were not allowing it to result in sinful actions as they had done with Joseph twenty-two years before.

It was also clear that they *did* care about their father and how their actions affected his physical and emotional well-being. And most of all, they had acknowledged their sin against God, followed by a deep and sincere repentance.

"HAVE EVERYONE LEAVE MY PRESENCE!"
Genesis 45:1,2

To this point Joseph had revealed very little emotion to his brothers. They had only observed him as a stern, rational Egyptian ruler. And at times when he could not mask his feelings he had left the room to weep in private. You can imagine what his brothers must have thought when they saw their accuser begin to lose emotional control and heard him cry out, "Have everyone leave my presence!" (Gen. 45:1).

Remember that at this moment they were on trial! They were being interrogated. Benjamin had been accused of stealing Joseph's silver cup. And Judah was pleading for mercy. From their perspective, Joseph's outburst would indicate that they were heading for serious trouble. It would appear that they had so angered this Egyptian official that he was either going to imprison them all for life or sentence them to death! There is no way that they could have interpreted Joseph's reaction as positive. They must have grimaced and withdrawn from his emotional outburst with intense fear.

Imagine too their reaction when this high-ranking official broke into violent sobs. He wept "so loudly" that the Egyptian attendants Joseph had ordered to leave the room could still hear what was happening (Gen. 45:2). From their perspective they may have reported to Pharaoh (Gen. 45:2) that their master had just gone insane, perhaps crumbling emotionally from the heavy task of directing the gigantic storehouse operation and the distribution of food.

But Joseph was far from a nervous breakdown. He had never been stronger and more mature. The pain he had felt all those years was behind him. He bore no serious emotional scars. And certainly what was transpiring at that moment would put the finishing touches on whatever healing he had needed. His tears were tears of relief and joy—not pain and suffering.

How long he wept uncontrollably we do not know, but this kind of emotional release takes time. The text implies that it continued long enough for the word to get back to "Pharaoh's household" through the servant grapevine.

We can also speculate from our own human experiences. Anyone who has ever encountered or personally experienced this kind of intense weeping knows that it does not last for a few minutes. These pent-up emotions in Joseph had built up, particularly over the last couple of months as he purposely hid his identity to gain answers to those important questions.

"I AM JOSEPH"
Genesis 45:3

Whatever time it took for Joseph to go through this therapeutic process, he finally gained sufficient control to tell them who he was. "I am Joseph!" he said. No doubt seeing their utter confusion and fear, he tried to put them at ease. He then asked a question that reflected his deep love and concern for his father, Jacob. It perhaps also reflected the fear he had experienced the last couple of months—fear that he may have contributed to his father's death by testing his brothers to determine their true motives and feelings. "*Is* my father still living?" he asked, evidently needing reassurance that he was, even though his brothers had answered that question affirmatively several times before (Gen. 43:27,28; 44:30-34).

Joseph's brothers were not prepared for what they were

hearing. They were so dumbfounded and overwhelmed with fear they could not respond. In fact, we're told specifically that "they were terrified," so much so they could not answer his question! (Gen. 45:3). They could not—they would not—believe what they were hearing and seeing. So long they had told the story of Joseph's death! So long they had believed he had been slain in Egypt! So long they had tried to hide their sins! Furthermore, a dead man cannot speak!

Though they could not respond overtly, several questions must have flashed through their minds. How would this Egyptian ruler know about Joseph? How would he know his name? Though they had alluded to Joseph, there is no evidence they had revealed his name. Furthermore, Joseph seemingly had never pursued the identity of the brother they had reported "no more" (Gen. 42:13). Though they had suspected that he was clairvoyant when he had seated them at the table according to their chronological age, at this moment they were utterly "terrified at his presence" (Gen. 45:3). If God had been punishing them for their sins through all of these Egyptian experiences—which they believed He was—then this was the ultimate judgment.

"COME CLOSE TO ME"
Genesis 45:4

Joseph could see they did not believe what he was saying. Though he was speaking perfect Hebrew, which probably frightened them even more, his appearance was Egyptian! To help convince them that he was indeed their brother, he asked them to "come close" to him (Gen. 45:4).

There is some speculation as to what happened at this moment. Was he simply asking them to draw near so he could look deep into their eyes, saying softly, "I *am* your brother Joseph, the *one* you sold into Egypt" (Gen. 45:4)?

Personally, I think not! Though it is a sensitive thought, it is a valid suggestion. In that private and intimate setting, some believe that Joseph opened his royal robe and revealed to them that he was like them. He too was circumcised, a mark of a true son of Abraham and something that set all of them apart from their pagan neighbors. No Egyptian man had that unique distinction. In fact, to them it would be a mark of disgrace to be like a Hebrew.

"DO NOT BE DISTRESSED AND DO NOT BE ANGRY"
Genesis 45:5

Whatever happened, they now believed. But predictably, their fear turned to distress and self-hatred. How could they face their brother? How could they have done what they had done? How could they have been so evil? Feelings of regret can be overwhelming and turn inward!

But Joseph, sensitive and perceptive man that he was, quickly discerned what was happening. He had never tested them to make them suffer but rather to discover the truth. And he did not want them to suffer now. "Do not be distressed" he pleaded. "Do not be angry with yourselves for selling me here." Then Joseph made a statement that must have overwhelmed them even more. "It was to save lives that God sent me ahead of you. . . . God sent me ahead of you to preserve for you a remnant on earth and to save your lives by a great deliverance" (Gen. 45:5,7).

"IT WAS NOT YOU WHO SENT ME HERE, BUT GOD"
Genesis 45:8

Joseph then concluded his explanation with a logical statement, "So then," he said, "it was not you who sent me here, but God" (Gen. 45:8).

We now have a very clear perception of Joseph's viewpoint on his suffering. At what point in time he had gained this spiritual insight, we're not told. But it must have begun to come clear when he first saw his brothers bowing before him and then remembered the dreams of his youth. And from that moment forward he began to plan for their welfare—especially the welfare of his father. In his heart he wanted to bring them to Egypt in order to protect and provide for them.

But how could he without knowing their spiritual condition? How could he without knowing how they felt about Jacob—and Benjamin? How they felt about them would be how they would still feel about him. There was no logical way he could justify his desire and plan to Pharaoh if indeed they had not changed. It would only have created havoc in his royal court—and eventually in all Egypt. It would have threatened the very position God had called him to fulfill. Furthermore, Pharaoh would never have had compassion on Joseph's brothers had he known the truth regarding what had happened—especially if their hearts had not changed.

Joseph, then, had to test them for their own sakes. He had to have answers to his questions, for he could never gain Pharaoh's permission without being convinced in his own heart they were different men.

But Joseph also knew he would have no difficulty making the decision to bring his family to Egypt if there had been repentance and reconciliation. In fact, he knew he had sufficient authority to make that decision himself and that Pharaoh would never question it. And once he was convinced he could trust them, he made that decision.

Joseph explained to his brothers how God had made him "father to Pharaoh, lord of his entire household and ruler of all Egypt" (Gen. 45:8). He instructed them to return to Canaan immediately and to explain to their father what had happened. He further instructed them to tell Jacob to come to Egypt post haste and he would provide for him a place in Goshen, and not only for him but for them, their children and their grandchildren, their flocks and their herds and everything that they owned (Gen. 45:9-11).

Following Joseph's instructions came one of the most

tender and beautiful scenes in all of Scripture. Joseph "threw his arms around his brother Benjamin and wept, and Benjamin embraced him, weeping." He then "kissed *all* his brothers and wept over them" (Gen. 45:14,15). And once they had been totally reunited in heart and spirit they sat together and *talked*—something they had probably not really done before in their lifetime.

"DON'T QUARREL ON THE WAY!"
Genesis 45:16-24

When Pharaoh found out what had happened, he "and all his officials were pleased" (Gen. 45:16). He approved Joseph's overall plan, but added some specifics of his own. "Bring your father and your families back to me," he said. "I will give you the best of the land of Egypt and you can enjoy the fat of the land." (Gen. 45:18). And he told them further not to bring any of their personal belongings because he would provide them with all new things—"the best of all Egypt" (Gen. 45:20). They were about to become the best dressed shepherds in the land.

Joseph wasted no time carrying out Pharaoh's orders. In fact, this was probably the first time in a long time Pharaoh had *told Joseph* what to do. How good it must have made Joseph feel to have the king's approval, cooperation and active participation. This is what he had hoped and prayed for all along. And now it was happening! In Pharaoh's mind, if these men were anything like Joseph, he saw them all as assets to his kingdom rather than liabilities. How ironical!

After loading the carts, giving them new clothes and providing them with provisions for the journey, Joseph sent them on their way. But his parting words are classic and seemingly tongue-in-cheek. In a teasing fashion, he must have said with a twinkle in his eyes and a smile on his face, "Don't quarrel on the way!" (Gen. 45:24).

A PERSPECTIVE

Have you noticed in this story how often Joseph wept? The *first* instance involved the conversation his brothers were having in his presence, not realizing he could understand Hebrew. Joseph had just informed them that one of them would be detained and put in custody while the others returned to Canaan to get Benjamin. It was at this point they began to perceive that their lives might be in serious jeopardy because of what they had done to Joseph twenty-two years earlier. "Surely," they said to one another, "we are being punished because of our brother. We saw how distressed he was when he pleaded with us for his life, but we would not listen" (Gen. 42:21).

Reuben then reminded them of his own warning at that time, "Didn't I tell you not to sin against the boy? But you wouldn't listen. Now we must give an accounting for his blood" (Gen. 42:22).

Though Joseph had been speaking Egyptian and using an interpreter, unknown to them he could understand every word they were saying. At that point he could not control his emotions. "He turned away from them and began to *weep*" (Gen. 42:24).

The *second* instance involved Joseph's first encounter with Benjamin when they returned from Canaan. "Deeply moved at the sight of his brother, Joseph hurried out and looked for a place to *weep*." Evidently he was so out of control that he eventually "went into his private room and *wept* there" (Gen. 43:30).

The *third* instance happened after Judah's repentant confession and his sincere request that he be allowed to take Benjamin's place as a slave so that their father Jacob would not suffer any more emotional pain. At this point, as we've seen, Joseph wept uncontrollably (Gen. 45:2).

The *fourth* instance involved the most touching scene thus far. It happened after Joseph revealed his identity and when his brothers really understood who he was and that he held no grudges. Furthermore, he revealed his plan to bring them all to Egypt to care for them. At that juncture, "he threw his arms around his brother Benjamin and *wept*, and Benjamin embraced him, *weeping*." And then, what may have been a *first* in their family experience, he "kissed all his brothers and *wept* over them" (Gen. 45:14,15).

There are three more instances of Joseph's weeping yet future in our story. When his father finally arrived in Egypt, we read that Joseph "threw his arms around his father and *wept* for a long time" (Gen. 46:29). And seventeen years later (Gen. 47:28), when Jacob died, we read that "Joseph threw himself upon his father and *wept* over him and kissed him (Gen. 50:1). And finally, after his father had died, his brothers were afraid Joseph might seek revenge. They sent a message to their brother that their father requested of Joseph before he died that he forgive them for their wrong-doing. "When their message came to him, Joseph *wept*" (Gen. 50:17).

What caused Joseph to weep in each of these instances? Obviously, there are similarities in each situation. But there are also some distinctive reasons.

In the *first* instance, he certainly wept because their conversation brought back some very painful memories. He remembered his own cries for mercy and how they turned their back on him and would not listen. But perhaps more so, he was emotionally touched because he heard them acknowledge their sin. Even though they were doing so because they were threatened it was a beginning point and Joseph responded with tears.

Joseph's tearful response tells us a great deal about his true perspective and heart, even in the early stages of the process of reconciliation. If he had been bitter and angry, he would have initially rejoiced over their predicament. He would have enjoyed seeing them squirm. If he were truly vindictive, he would have turned away with a smirk, perhaps even laughing. Rather, he cried!

In the *second* instance, Joseph wept because he was reunited with his brother Benjamin. For years he had wondered how his brothers had been treating him, no doubt envisioning the possibility that they had actually done the same thing to his little brother that they had done to him. He rejoiced because Benjamin was still alive and well. And though he said, "God be gracious to you, my son" (Gen. 43:29), he perhaps meant in his heart—"God *has* been gracious to you, my son."

In the *third* instance, Joseph wept because he saw in his brothers true repentance, and particularly in Judah's heart and life. He saw his older brother bearing the responsibility for what happened, and more so, showing deep concern for their father and how keeping Benjamin as a slave would affect this old man's emotional and physical health—perhaps even causing his death.

In the *fourth* instance, Joseph wept because he was reconciled with his brothers, communicating with them in his mother tongue. They were tears of rejoicing.

The *fifth* and *sixth* instances are common reasons for tears. joseph was reunited with his father whom he loved very much. This probably was the most painful separation of all, and to once again be with him was a great cause for rejoicing in Joseph's heart. And the sixth reason—his father's death—is probably one of the most common reasons for weeping in every culture of the world.

The final reason reveals Joseph's heart of compassion. He *had* forgiven them and it grieved him that they were still suffering from guilt and fear.

SOME PERSONAL REFLECTIONS

1. God created human beings with a capacity to weep. As God's children we have many capacities. One of the most important is that we can cry. It is a God-created means for emotional release. Research shows, in fact, that people who lose loved ones in death and who do not allow them-

selves to weep at some point in time are probably headed for some future emotional struggles. In some instances it may result in psychological depression or perhaps anger and bitterness. Let's remember that when Jesus arrived in Bethany following the death of Lazarus, He—the Son of God—"wept" (John 11:35). God Himself then is modeling for us that it's all right to weep. After all, He made us that way.

2. Weeping is not necessarily a sign of weakness. It can also be a mark of great strength. In our culture, weeping—on the part of men particularly—is often considered a weakness. That is an interesting conclusion in the light of our story of Joseph. No one who has a correct view of this man would ever classify him as being weak. He endured the most hurtful of all experiences—rejection by his own brothers—and he emerged stronger than ever. He did not allow bitterness to consume his being or to interfere with his ability to think clearly and to act responsibly. Consequently he rose to a position of great prominence in Egypt. Furthermore, in the process he did not allow rejection and anger nor human temptation, to drive him to an illegitimate sexual relationship when the opportunity *more* than presented itself. Nor did he use his position of power to retaliate when the opportunity came. This represents a man of great emotional and spiritual strength, not weakness.

And yet Joseph often wept. I suppose the instances we read about are only a few compared with the numerous times he must have cried himself to sleep, particularly in the early years of separation. So, men, don't let pride keep you from doing what God says is normal. When you hurt, don't be afraid to weep. The facts are, it's your weakness that may be keeping you from expressing your emotions in this way.

I remember a big, strong football player who walked into our church one day. He used to be quarterback for Southern Methodist University. His name was "Rusty"

Russell. He had just come into a personal relationship with Christ. He used to sit in church listening to the Word of God and to people share what Christ meant to them. Almost every Sunday following his conversion to Christ, big tears would fill his eyes and often flow down his cheeks. One day he said to a friend of mine, "You know, before I became a Christian I *never* cried—not *once*. Now, I cry almost every Sunday!"

3. There is a time and place to weep and it's to be done with proper motives. Joseph certainly demonstrates this lesson. If he had been immature in his reactions he would have allowed himself to lose control in front of his brothers much sooner, which in turn would have interfered with what he knew he had to do to get answers to his questions. Consequently, when he could not control himself he went to a private place.

Joseph also illustrates another point. He did not use weeping as a means of manipulation. In our culture, men often do not weep because they are proud and insecure. On the other hand, since crying is more natural for women, some—certainly not all—develop the *art* of weeping. The reasons of course are frequently to achieve personal and selfish goals!

Weeping is a normal means to express emotions, but if we use it with false motives we'll not only hurt ourselves in the end but confuse others. Eventually people will not take us seriously if we "cry" wolf too often.

4. Weeping often clears the way for objective communication. Note that after Joseph wept with his brothers they spent time talking (Gen. 45:15). Again, this may have been a first-time experience from the standpoint of mature and open communication.

Often crying *does* enable people to communicate more effectively. Emotional layers are peeled back so we can be more objective and authentic. Furthermore, we can relate at a less serious level, even laughing at ourselves and our weaknesses. This seems to have happened when Joseph told his brothers not to quarrel on their way back to Canaan (Gen. 45:24). It hardly seems logical that he would be seriously admonishing them at this juncture. Rather, they seemed to be able to look at the mistakes and sins of the past and even inject some humor. This is often the true test of reconciliation—particularly when deep pain has been involved.

5. Weeping can be a true test of our motives. Joseph wept because of some very noble reasons. In summary he wept:

• Because he saw his brothers' hearts begin to soften in their relationship to God.

• Because his brother Benjamin had not suffered the same plight he had suffered.

• Because he saw Judah's true concern for his father, Jacob.

• Because he was reconciled with his brothers.

• Because he was reunited with his father whom he loved deeply.

• Because his father died.

• Because of grief caused by his brothers' lingering guilt.

A PERSONAL CHALLENGE

Stop and think for a moment:

When was the last time you wept?

NOTE: If it has been a long time, perhaps (but not necessarily) you're bottling up and overly suppressing your emotions. This may be particularly true if you're a man.

Why have you wept?

NOTE: Can you check any of the following? If you can, you can identify with Joseph and be sure you have wept for some very noble reasons.

☐ Because you've seen people respond spiritually

☐ Because another person has been spared suffering

☐ Because you've seen someone deeply concerned for someone else

☐ Because you've been truly reconciled with someone who has mistreated you

☐ Because you've been reunited with a loved one or a dear friend

☐ Because of the death of a loved one or close friend

☐ Because you are grieved over another person's emotional pain.

12

Joseph's
Final Years

GENESIS 45:25-50:26

• Why do some people have difficulty accepting the fact
they have been forgiven—both by God and others they
have hurt or offended?

• How can we explain the fact that God can even take evil
and make it work out for good?

• When God does turn evil into good, who is responsible
for the evil?

When Joseph's brothers returned from Egypt and told
their aged father that Joseph was still alive, his initial
response—understandably—was one of disbelief. He "was
stunned" (Gen. 45:26)! His sons had to either be thor-
oughly confused or outright lying. After all those years of
thinking that Joseph had been torn to pieces by a wild animal, Jacob could not respond with hope. The memory of

his son's blood-stained ornamental robe must have flashed through his mind, as it had a thousand times over the twenty-two year period.

But the more his sons talked and shared what Joseph had said, "and when he saw the carts Joseph had sent to carry him back," his spirit revived (Gen. 45:27). It had to be true. There was too much evidence. Jacob must have sensed sincerity in his sons as never before. They were different men. Furthermore, where would they have gotten so many things—their new clothing and the twenty donkeys "loaded with grain and bread" (Gen. 45:23)?

Benjamin's affirmation would be the most convincing. There he stood, verifying his brother's story, wearing brand new clothes with five additional sets in his arms. And you can imagine Jacob's emotional response when Benjamin unloaded his bags of silver—300 shekels in all—fifteen times the amount exchanged between the Midianites and Joseph's brothers when he was sold into Egypt.

"I'm convinced!" Jacob cried out. "My son Joseph *is* still alive. I will go and see him before I die" (Gen. 45:28).

A GRAND REUNION
Genesis 46:1-4,28,29

As soon as they could get everything together, Jacob left for Egypt with his sons and their families. On the way he stopped in Beersheba and "offered sacrifices" to God (Gen. 46:1). There the Lord spoke to him directly and affirmed what his sons had shared with him, and assured him of His personal presence with Jacob as he traveled to Egypt. And you can imagine his elation when God told him that "Joseph's own hand" would close his eyes when he died (Gen. 46:4).

Joseph was waiting anxiously for his dad's arrival. And what a reunion it was! Traveling to Goshen he met Jacob there and "threw his arms around his father and wept for a long time" (Gen. 46:29). When Jacob finally gained enough emotional control to speak coherently, with what must have been a quivering voice—affected both by his age as well as the intense emotion of that glorious moment, he uttered: "Now I am ready to die, since I have seen for myself that you are still alive" (Gen. 46:30).

But a revived spirit does marvelous things to a human being, even at age 130. Jacob lived another seventeen years and did not die until age 147 (Gen. 47:28). How much he must have enjoyed that period of time, which almost equalled the years he had been separated from Joseph, and equalled exactly the years he had spent with Joseph before he was sold into Egypt. Furthermore, he spent those years in luxury, living in a section of Egypt unequalled in productivity. As Pharaoh promised, Jacob and his sons and their families settled in "the best of the land of Egypt" where they could "enjoy the fat of the land" (Gen. 45:18).

Jacob also enjoyed the unique and unexpected pleasure of fellowship with Joseph's children. What a delightful surprise to this old man who firmly believed he would never see his son Joseph again—let alone Joseph's children. Shortly before Jacob died, while blessing Joseph's sons Manasseh and Ephraim, he stated, "I never expected to see your face again, but now God has allowed me to see your children too" (Gen. 48:11).

A ROYAL FUNERAL
Genesis 49:29-50:1-9

Just before Jacob died he asked that his body be taken back to Canaan so he could be buried in the same place as his grandfather, Abraham, and his father, Isaac. When Pharaoh heard about Jacob's desire, he granted Joseph permission to honor his father's final request. In fact, he treated Jacob as if he were an Egyptian dignitary. He had all of his officials accompany Joseph, including the "dignitaries of his court and *all* the dignitaries of Egypt" (Gen. 50:7). He also sent with them "chariots and horsemen"—all in all "a very large company" (Gen. 50:9).

What a tremendous parade of people this must have been! And think how Joseph must have felt. Seeing his father honored in this way would have made his past problems and pain worth it all. Remember too, that by honoring Jacob in this way, Pharaoh was in actuality honoring Joseph. It was Joseph's faithfulness to the king and his reputation in Egypt that caused Pharaoh to bestow upon Jacob such royal treatment.

A FINAL PERSPECTIVE
Genesis 50:15-26

Though Joseph was certainly rejoicing in Pharaoh's thoughtfulness and feeling a deep sense of gratitude as they were traveling back to Canaan to bury his father, his brothers on the other hand were deeply troubled. Their fear was triggered when Jacob died. A nagging question kept going through their minds: "What if Joseph holds a grudge against us and pays us back for all the wrongs we did to him?" (Gen. 50:15).

The Problem of Projection

Guilt has a way of lingering even though we're told we're forgiven. Furthermore, they knew Joseph's deep love for their father and that he would have done nothing to send the old man to an early grave. Though they had been assured by Joseph both with words and actions that he had no animosity in his heart towards them, they began to experience deep anxiety when their father passed off the scene.

To understand their fear, we need to also understand how easy it is for people who have mistreated others to interpret another person's actions in light of their own weaknesses. How could Joseph have forgiven them for what they had done? He couldn't be sincere and for real. He must be feigning forgiveness to protect Jacob. His acts of unselfishness in bringing them all to Egypt and bestowing upon them such rich blessings *must* have been to honor their father and to make up for all the heartache he had endured and they had caused for twenty-two years! No man is capable of overlooking such grievous ill treatment without retaliation!

Why would Joseph's brothers think this way? The answer is simple. They could not have demonstrated the same attitudes and actions themselves. Consequently, they projected on Joseph their own weaknesses! And so it has been ever since Adam and Eve introduced sin into the world. People have difficulty trusting others because of their own weaknesses. From their own experiential vantage point, Jacob's sons would naturally conclude that their brother Joseph could not be that forgiving. There must be another motive. Knowing Joseph's love for their father they concluded that he was the reason for their own royal treatment. Now that Jacob was gone they braced themselves for retaliation.

A Two-Fold Strategy (Gen. 50:16-18)

These men needed reassurance and their strategy was two-fold. Since they feared Joseph's love and respect for Jacob may have been the reason he had not retaliated, they used that very love and respect as a basis of intercession. They sent word to Joseph that their father had left instructions before he died requesting that he forgive his brothers "the sins and the wrongs they committed" against him (Gen. 50:17).

The biblical text is not clear as to whether or not this was something they conjured up after Jacob died or if they in fact had gone to their father while he was still alive. If they were fabricating a story out of fear, Joseph would certainly have discerned it, and perhaps this explains his own response.

When Joseph received their message he again revealed his own sensitive heart. He *had* forgiven them—long ago, even before they originally came to Egypt. He had *never* planned to retaliate, even *before* they acknowledged their sins. And again his heart was touched by their own inner anxiety and fear. Once again he could not hold back the tears. He did not want them to continue punishing themselves because of their wrongdoing (Gen. 50:17). But perhaps Joseph was also revealing his own heart because of their inability to trust him, even after he had demonstrated so much love for them the last seventeen years.

Joseph's brothers then took their second self-protective step. They followed their father's message with a personal appearance before Joseph. Once again they "threw themselves down before him" and said, "We are your slaves" (Gen. 50:18). This action on their part represented a very sincere effort to placate Joseph should he still be angry, for he had certainly not treated them as slaves the last seventeen years. Rather, they had been treated more like royalty—which may have in reality actually accentuated their guilt problem.

Joseph's Balanced Response (Gen. 50:19-21)

Joseph's response represents one of the most mature viewpoints expressed in all Scripture. He combined a human perspective with a divine outlook on what had happened. On the one hand he was sensitive to their fears and anxieties. He knew they were human and identified with their anguish. "Don't be afraid," he said (Gen. 50:19). Joseph was reiterating what he had said the day he had revealed his identity seventeen years earlier. At that time he told them not to "be distressed" nor "angry" with themselves. And once again "he reassured them and spoke kindly to them" (Gen. 50:19). He could not and would not retaliate.

Joseph then reiterated *why* he would not retaliate. It's obvious, first of all, from his life's story, that he was just not that kind of man. He did not harbor bitterness. But even more basic than his gentle spirit and natural compassion was the fact that his *theology* affected his attitudes and actions. He knew that it was *God's* prerogative to vindicate His servants for sin committed against them. And Joseph made that perspective clear when he asked them a pointed but rhetorical questions: "Am I in the place of God?" (Gen. 50:19).

In this sense Joseph was an Old Testament Paul, modeling what he wrote hundreds of years later. "Do not repay anyone evil for evil" (Rom. 12:17). "Do not take revenge, my friends, but leave room for God's wrath" (Rom. 12:19). Though I'm sure Joseph was tempted at times to use his position of power to deliberately get even, his divine perspective would not allow him to do so.

At this point in time, Joseph's perspective was also quite clear and complete. He saw God's hand in it all. Though there were times during that period in Egypt when he had to trust God in the midst of total darkness and total confusion, he now understood why he had been sold into Egypt. He had also stated that reason the day he revealed his identity (Gen. 45:5-8). But he knew he must reiterate it once again with even greater insight and wisdom. Seventeen years before he made no reference to the evil part they had played in it all. The focus was on God's sovereign plan for his life as well as theirs. "It was to save lives that *God* sent me ahead of you" he had said (Gen. 45:5). Elaborating, he continued—"*God* sent me ahead of you to preserve you for a remnant on earth and to save your lives by a great deliverance. So then," he concluded, "it was not you who sent me here, but God" (Gen. 45:7,8).

The facts are, however, that they *had* sinned exceedingly in doing what they had done. They *had* sold him into Egypt. A divine perspective is not enough to deal with sin—especially when you are a part of it. And it seems that Joseph sensed their need to hear him acknowledge that what they had done was indeed wrong. And so he did! He continued, "You intended to harm me, but God intended it for good to accomplish what is now being done, the saving of many lives" (Gen. 50:20).

Yes, his brothers *had* sinned. What they had done *was* an evil deed. And they had intended it to be evil. They hated Joseph with *intense* hatred. And what they had done was also a sin against their father, Jacob. They had lied and in doing so they had caused him twenty-three years of deep, emotional agony. Consequently, they had suffered for their sins, for they had spent twenty-three years with guilty consciences, reminded daily of what they had done by their father's grief-stricken countenance. And now, seventeen years later, they were still suffering the natural consequences of their sins.

But beyond it all, God had used Joseph's experiences to accomplish His divine purposes. The brothers' evil actions served as a means to save their lives and to allow God to fulfill His promises to Abraham that he would bless him, his son Isaac, and his grandson Jacob—and all mankind with a great nation that would eventually provide a Saviour for the world, Jesus Christ our Lord (Gen. 12:1-3). Though Joseph may not have understood it all, he understood enough to see a divine pattern in the evil as well as the good. That, of course, *is* a mature perspective.

And Joseph had that perspective until the day he died. Calling his brothers together one day, he said: " 'I am about to die. But God will surely come to your aid and take you up out of this land to the land he promised on oath to Abraham, Isaac and Jacob.' And Joseph made the sons of Israel swear an oath and said, 'God will surely come to your aid, and then you must carry my bones up from this place' " (Gen. 50:24,25).

At that point "Joseph died at the age of a hundred and ten." As "they embalmed him" and as "he was placed in a coffin in Egypt" (Gen. 50:26) they laid to rest an Old Testament great who exemplifies in a marvelous way a man who lived for God with all his heart in the good times as well as the bad. He is indeed a great model and example for us all.

SOME PERSONAL REFLECTIONS

Our personal theology should make a difference as to how we face difficult circumstances. We're all human beings, just like Joseph. And even though God had a very unusual and special purpose for allowing suffering in his life, we also can claim Romans 8:28 for our lives.

First, this does *not* mean that we will *not* be tempted to hurt those who hurt us. If we're human at all we'll be tempted to look for opportunities to get even. If we find ourselves in a position of power over those who hurt us, we will probably be tempted even more to retaliate and take vengeance.

At that point we must decide to *do* what is right, not what we *feel* like doing. At that moment we must rely on God to help us do His will. If vengeance is necessary, *God* will do it. "It is mine to revenge," the Lord said. "I will repay" (Rom 12:19). Our part is to feed our enemy and to give him something to drink. We are to overcome evil by doing good (Rom. 12:21). Joseph's life illustrates this beautifully.

This does not mean we should relate to someone who has not repented and who continues to do evil as if nothing has happened. Joseph faced that problem as well. There was no way he could bring his brothers to Egypt and provide for them without knowing that their hearts were changed. It would have been devastating for them and others as well. But the fact remains that Joseph's precautions were *not* motivated by anger and a desire to take vengeance on his brothers but by that which was best for his father, his brothers and the kingdom he served.

This represents a fine line. Motives are often difficult to discern. But there are inner clues that help us. And Joseph illustrates one of the most significant clues. His heart was soft and compassionate, not hard and unfeeling, reflecting pride and arrogance. This is why he so often wept.

2. People who do wrong and yet see God's purpose in allowing it, must never excuse their sin as being caused by God. How easy that would be, especially if we wanted to rationalize our wrongdoing while contemplating a sinful action or *after* we have actually participated in the sin. There are some who could read the story of Joseph and his brothers and be tempted to blame God for their sin.

James warned against this kind of thinking when he wrote, "When tempted, no one should say 'God is tempting me.' For God cannot be tempted by evil, nor does he tempt anyone; but each one is tempted when, by his own evil desire, he is dragged away and enticed. Then, after desire has conceived, it gives birth to sin; and sin, when it is full-grown, gives birth to death (Jas. 1:13-15).

3. Not all human problems and pain can be explained by Joseph's experience. Joseph's experience was unique. God had a very special plan in mind in allowing his suffering. In retrospect, Joseph could see a very special purpose.

There are times Christians suffer, however, that are not as easily explained. For example, how do we explain rape to a person marred for life? Or how do we explain child abuse that leaves an individual an emotional cripple? Or how do we explain mental torture that drives a person insane? Or how do we rationalize the ravages of war that leave thousands of people maimed for life?

We must realize that suffering in general is related to the fact that the world is contaminated by sin. And this affects us all. Though He certainly could, God seemingly chooses at times not to involve Himself directly in what happens. He has given mankind free will, and with that free will, any individual can reject God's claim on his life for protection or Lordship. Just so, anyone can act out his sinful nature in hurtful ways.

There are two dimensions to this problem. First, we can

use our freedom and make others suffer. Second, we can use that freedom and cause severe suffering in our own lives. And usually both dimensions are interrelated.

Adolph Hitler certainly is an example of the first dimension. Under his leadership, millions of innocent people experienced excruciating suffering, often leading to horrible death. No one would conclude that God directed Hitler to do what he did. He did what he did because he had a free will, and he deliberately used his freedom to hurt others and make them suffer.

On the other hand, many people suffer because of the consequences of sin in their own lives. Paul stated that "a man reaps what he sows. The one who sows to please his sinful nature, from that nature will reap destruction" (Gal. 6:7,8).

Many people, then, suffer because of a world polluted by sin. In explaining that suffering, we can only go back to the fact that man is basically sinful, and if he allows his evil nature to take over, he'll hurt other people in the process, as well as himself.

4. Though suffering may be difficult to explain, and the reason for it is not clear, a Christian has the potential to see good result in spite of suffering or because of it.

This is the truth of Romans 8:28. Paul wrote, "And we know that in all things God works for the good of those who love him, who have been called according to his purpose."

Following are some of the purposes God can accomplish in our lives and in the lives of others when we suffer:

• We may have opportunities to communicate the gospel of Christ. When Paul was in prison in Rome, he wrote to the Philippians and told them that what was happening to him was really serving "to advance the gospel" (Phil. 1:12). And this had been true in the lives of many Christians who have suffered persecution over the years. They have turned it into an opportunity to witness for Jesus Christ.

• Personal suffering helps us to understand the sufferings of others. Paul clearly illustrates this purpose in his second letter to the Corinthians. "Praise be to the God and Father of our Lord Jesus Christ, the Father of compassion and the God of all comfort," he wrote, "who comforts us in all our troubles, so that we can comfort those in any trouble with the comfort we ourselves have received from God" (2 Cor. 1:3,4).

On a number of occasions when I have been counseling those who have experienced unusual suffering through no particular fault of their own, I've often emphasized the fact that if they can view their problems with a positive attitude, God can use them in a special way to minister to others who are going through the same distress. No one can understand a rape victim like a person who has been raped. No one can understand the bitterness and the anxiety that is caused in a child's life because of divorce like a person who has gone through that particular trauma. No one can understand a person who has gone through child abuse and suffered the consequences like a person who has gone through the experience. God can use these negative experiences to be positive influences in other people's lives.

• Suffering can produce Christian maturity. James wrote that Christians should "consider it pure joy" when they "face trials of many kinds." He then states the reason: "Because you know that the testing of your faith develops perseverance. Perseverance must finish its work so that you may be mature and complete, not lacking anything" (Jas. 1:2-4).

• Suffering can bring an individual to a salvation experience. Suffering has always been the occasion for some individuals inviting Jesus Christ to be their Saviour. Without coming to the place of helplessness, they may never have turned to God for help. Better to suffer in this life than to spend all eternity separated from God!

• Beyond all this, of course, there is suffering that we

cannot understand at all. This is particularly true when a righteous person undergoes severe trials. It is difficult to see a reason, let alone a purpose. Job had this kind of experience. He trusted God even when all others had turned away from him—even his wife, who advised him to "curse God and die" (Job. 2:9).

But because Job knew God in a personal way, he also knew that beyond this life he would understand. He saw meaning in his suffering, even though it had to be based on the fact that God is a God who will ultimately make all things clear.

Relative to this kind of problem, I am reminded of Victor Frankl, who endured the ravishes of a Nazi concentration camp. Dr. Frankl, a psychiatrist and a Jew, was taken captive by the Nazis. Because he was in good health, he was among those who had to work long hours in the mine fields. Those who were not healthy were ushered immediately to the gas chambers.

People all around him were dying. He too was rapidly losing hope. With every day, his body got weaker and his ability to cope deteriorated rapidly.

One morning when the guards came to rouse all the prisoners, Dr. Frankl could hardly drag himself from his cot. Given a crust of bread, he joined the others as they plodded across the frozen soil, headed for the fields. As he walked he felt he was literally going to die. But at that moment he began to think of his philosophy of helping others. Over the years he had developed a system of counseling called *logo therapy*. Literally, this word means to help a person see *meaning* in crisis and suffering.

But what meaning could he possibly see in what was happening? As he trudged along, struggling between life and death, he finally gained enough emotional energy to see himself with his mind's eye lecturing in an auditorium filled with people. The subject was "How I Endured the Ravages of a Nazi Concentration Camp by Seeing Meaning in Suffering." The meaning he was referring to was the fact that he could stand before these people and tell them that his therapy really worked.

Through his experience of being able to project in his mind this possibility, he gained enough courage to make it through the day. He then made another day, and another, until eventually the war was over and he was released.

The sequel to this story is very personal. Several years ago, my wife and I attended a lecture at the University of Dallas. There we heard Dr. Frankl tell this story. What he had seen in his mind's eye, which gave him strength to endure the suffering, was being fulfilled before our very eyes. There he stood, lecturing on the subject of how he had indeed endured the ravages of a Nazi concentration camp by seeing this particular meaning in his suffering.

As I sat and listened, my heart was deeply moved. Here was a man who may not have known Jesus Christ personally. However, he had discovered some very important principles that Jesus Christ taught. They worked even for him. As I thought about this, the point became clear. If the principle inherent in Romans 8:28 will work for those who do not claim to be Christians in the biblical sense of that word, then what about those of us who really do know Jesus Christ in a personal way? How much more should we be able to see meaning in suffering, even though we may not be able to even understand its purpose?

A PERSONAL CHALLENGE

Review the practical lessons in each chapter.

1. List those that have been most meaningful to you.

2. List in order of priority those you need to apply to your life right now.

3. Turn these lessons into personal goals.

4. Make each goal a matter of prayer.

5. Write out what practical steps you can take to reach these goals.

6. Begin today to apply your first goal.